The Anxiety Shift - Gut Rehab

By Neil Breakwell

The information in this book is true and complete to the best of my knowledge. This book is intended only as an informative guide for those wishing to know more about health issues. In no way is this book intended to replace, countermand, or conflict with the advice given to you by your own physician. The ultimate decision concerning care should be made between you and your doctor. I strongly recommend you follow his or her advice. Information in this book is general and is offered with no guarantees on the part of the author. The author disclaims all liability relating to the use of this book.

Second Edition

This second edition contains a few minor changes to the content, specifically the layout of the citations and a few grammar tweaks. The cover has also been updated just to try and keep things a bit fresh, but most importantly my name has changed. The first editions of both books in this series were written under my pen name of Neil Gabriel. The reason I used a pen name was because being a teacher in Thailand led to a lot of students Googling my name, and I did not really want them or the school knowing that I wrote about anxiety in my spare time. I was also unsure how the government would view the whole thing in relation to my work permit. So, I used Neil Gabriel. Now that I am no longer teaching in Thailand, and am currently working for a hotel in Vietnam, I decided to use my real name for the first time. That is why I decided to release this second edition of the book penned by Neil Breakwell.

I should also point out, that while I stand behind everything that I have said in this book, and most of it has been confirmed again and again by studies since I first started writing this in 2013, I now have a wider view of anxiety as a whole and view the gut as one part of a three-part root cause of anxiety. I still believe it is a very important, and often overlooked, part though, and while my third book builds a model based on these three parts, I still recommend this book to help people tackle their gut issues.

Contents

Preface

As you may have gathered from the title of this book, its main aim is to tackle anxiety. The difference between this book and most other anxiety books, though, is that this one requires a *shift* in the traditional thinking of anxiety. It attacks anxiety from a completely different direction.

Traditionally, anxiety has always been considered a solely mental illness, with its causes, triggers, and symptoms all originating only in the mind. Now while this is certainly true for much of the catastrophizing, ruminating, and misinterpretations often associated with anxiety and panic disorders, it struck me as being an incomplete view on how anxiety gets started in the first place and how it can affect so many people for so long.

While most medical professionals will try to explain anxiety in terms of sensitization, the fight or flight response, or the ill-proportioned symptoms of worry and nervousness, very few (if any) can give a strong and valid argument for how it begins. They may have theories of course—theories that are usually based around ideas like trigger points or traumas in the past, chemical imbalances in the brain, genetic heredity, or learned traits that are developed in the environment of our formative years—but they don't really know. Now while this is not necessarily their fault, as it is undoubtedly a very complex issue, it is the very fact that it is so complicated, that I find it a little short sighted to believe that it can only possibly be a problem that is restricted to the mind.

The brain itself is, after all, a physical entity within the body—it uses solely physical processes (essentially electro-chemical reactions) to generate what we call thoughts, feelings, and emotions. Is it really beyond the scope of reality, then, that the brain could be affected by something else within the body? Could there be other physical processes that can modify these electro-chemical reactions to induce anxiety? I mean, there are plenty of people, and I was one of them, who suffer from waves of constant anxious feelings which seem to have no bearing on negative mental thoughts except to induce them. Is it at all possible that much of the anxiety in our minds has its origins in completely different parts of our body? I thought it worth finding out.

That is why, this book is taking a fresh perspective on the whole anxiety idea and applying the latest scientific research, and studies on anxiety, to develop a whole new theory on how anxiety begins and, more importantly of course, how you can tackle it. Not only will I give you the theory, and the scientific studies that back that theory up, but I will also give you a step-by-step process that will help put you on the road to beating your anxiety once and for all.

What makes this anxiety beating formula different to all the others that you have seen is that it stops treating anxiety as just a mental illness and treats it as a symptom of problems with both the mind and the body. It is these physical causes of anxiety that sets this book apart from the rest. It is these physical causes that most people are missing because they don't know they are there. That is why, in this book, I am going to give you a full system for beating anxiety based on this well-researched and centralised physical cause.

Although it might seem a little strange to some people, the idea that an illness that was thought to reside solely in the mind might have a physical cause and can be beaten through physical means should not come as too much of a surprise. As I said, the brain really is still a physical part of the body, and even when you take medication for mental illnesses, they all work by treating the physiological processes of the brain. Whether it is (supposedly) changing the rate at which serotonin is re-absorbed by the brain like SSRIs (Zoloft, Lexapro), or altering the rate at which neurons communicate through epinephrine like SNRIs (Effexor, Cymbalta), they all use physical processes to combat the anxiety symptoms. If medication can do it in the short-term, then who's to say healing physical issues with the body can't beat anxiety in the long term?

Anxiety certainly isn't the first illness that was thought to be caused by mental triggers but turned out to have a more physical root cause. For almost the entire 20th century, the lowly but extremely painful peptic ulcer was thought to be caused by stress— a manifestation of worry and anxiety. It was treated for decades with bed rest and hospitalisation. It wasn't until 1982 when Australian physicians, Robin Warren, and Barry Marshall, identified the culprit as the *Helicobacter pylori (H. pylori)* bacterium that attitudes started to change[1]. It was a seemingly innocuous bacterium in the gut that had been causing the problem all along.

Unfortunately, the medical establishment, it seems, takes a while to accept changes to previously accepted knowledge. In fact, even by 1995, long after it had been proven and accepted that H. pylori caused more than 90% of duodenal ulcers and up to 80% of

---

[1] Heliobacter Pylori (book) – Suzuki, Warren, Marshall [2016]

gastric ulcers, almost 90% of ulcer patients still believed that their ulcers were caused by stress or worry, and around 75% were being given completely the wrong medication.

I wouldn't expect the accepted ideas about anxiety to change anytime soon either, but it doesn't mean we shouldn't try.

Of course, to be completely free of anxiety and panic disorders you must treat the body and the mind together. Panic attacks certainly are a creation of the mind, and anxiety itself does, by its very nature, revolve around negative thoughts and beliefs. This is why I am a firm believer in a two-step system. The first step is to heal the body to remove the underlying physical anxiety triggers, and the second step is to correct any wrong thoughts that may have made their way into the mind during anxious episodes and could keep your anxiety alive.

This book is going to take care of the first step for you.

Although maybe a little far-fetched, I sometimes liken this two-step system to quitting smoking (mostly because I am well versed with quitting smoking and understand the difficulties). To quit smoking effectively you need to approach it in two stages: The first stage is to get through the initial physical dependency, so the body stops craving the nicotine, and the second is to beat the mental habits that have developed over years of smoking cigarettes—the associations that the brain makes between times and places and lighting up.

Now I'm certainly not saying that beating anxiety is on a par with quitting smoking, I am just using it as an analogy of a two-step system that involves both mind and body, and hoping it helps you visualise the need for two steps. The reason why there are over 40 million people still suffering from anxiety in the United States is because the only options available to them are to treat the mind or take medication, and neither has an overly impressive record in the long term on its own.

What is needed is a permanent solution for treating the body that will silence those anxiety triggers for good, and then you can finally start working on the mind. This book is going to show you how you can fix these problems with your body (that you probably aren't even aware you have) that are helping to keep your anxiety "switched on", so you can finally switch them off forever.

Once you reset your body, the rest becomes a million times easier. Once your body is fixed, your general feelings of anxiety, those overriding feelings of dread and doom, and the sensations of unreality and detachment should be gone, or at least drastically reduced. All you need to do then is tackle the mind through therapy or some simple CBT-style techniques (which incidentally you can find in the second book of The Anxiety Shift series).

Introduction

Since you are reading this book, I think it would be safe to assume that you or someone close to you suffers from some sort of anxiety disorder, or related issue, and would like to find a way to get rid of it. The first thing you need to know is that you are not alone: Over 40 million people in the United States alone suffer from anxiety-related illnesses. This is a huge number, and a number that is steadily increasing, even though billions of dollars every year are spent on drugs and supplements trying to fight it.

There are around 7 million people in the US that suffer from what is known as General Anxiety Disorder (GAD), and if you are one of these people, you will know what a nightmare it can be to be anxious about everything all the time. Your friends and co-workers may think of you as a "catastrophizer", because you always imagine the worst possible outcome to everything you do. You also might experience some of the common symptoms of GAD, such as fatigue, irritability, headaches, twitching, trembling, insomnia, muscle tension and a shortness of breath. Of course, GAD is not the only anxiety disorder to plague millions of people—there is also social anxiety disorder, health anxiety disorder, panic disorder, and agoraphobia (as well as PTSD, OCD etc.)

The problem is, of course, that it is not fully understood what causes these anxiety disorders, and many doctors do not know how to deal with patients who suffer from them resulting in a slew of drug prescriptions aimed at tackling the symptoms rather than the root cause. This is music to the ears of big pharmaceutical companies who are more than happy to churn out medicines that only mask symptoms in customers, as this keeps them customers for life. This is much more profitable than finding a cure.

This may sound cynical, but I am sure if you have been on the merry-go-round of anxiety treatments for any amount of time, you will understand where this cynicism comes from. Because of the associated "life sentence" and the possible side effects that accompany anxiety medication, I do not believe that medication is the best course of action for anxiety sufferers. I believe tackling the problem at its root-cause is the best way to eliminate anxiety, and if there is a chance that you could be anxiety free with no expensive drugs, no nasty side effects, and no regular doctor visits, wouldn't you at least want to give it a try too?

Before we begin, I have three questions for you, three questions that you may never have been asked in relation to your anxiety before: *Do you have any digestive issues like diarrhoea, constipation, or bloating? Do you suffer from acid reflux? Have you noticed any change in your digestion before or since the onset of your anxiety?*

Now these questions might seem strange, and if the answer to all three is no, don't worry, that certainly does not mean that this book cannot help you, but if the answer to at least one of these questions is yes, then you are experiencing what originally drove me to write this book in the first place, and what I now believe is a root cause of the anxiety epidemic—the relationship between an unhealthy gut and anxiety.

My aim in this book is to demonstrate that there is a clear and definite link between the gut and anxiety, and even if you do not display symptoms of any digestive disorder, there is still a good chance that your anxiety is caused by (or at the very least worsened by) a problem or imbalance within your gut. Once I have (hopefully) established that anxiety can be a direct consequence of a gut disorder, I will offer solutions to help you tackle your gut disorder, and hence your anxiety, in the most suitable fashion for you.

A little About Me

Before I tell you about myself there is just one thing I want to get out of the way: I am not a doctor, and I have never been a doctor, and I am in no way qualified to give medical advice. That said, I don't consider this to necessarily be a bad thing. I am certainly not against doctors, in fact, my brother is a doctor, and my mother was a nurse and a counsellor, but it must be said that the medical establishment can sometimes be a little reluctant in accepting new ideas and theories, and it can take a lifetime or more for hypotheses to make it to the medical journals.

This of course is how it should be. Doctors must be 100% confident that something works before they recommend it to their patients, as they have their reputations, their livelihoods, and the welfare of their patients to protect. This means they will often give little time to theories[2] that have not made it into their books. This is not true for all doctors of course, but I have found it to be the case with most.

It also depends, of course, how much each individual doctor keeps up to date with their peer reviewed journals and latest

____

[2] When I use the word "theory" here, I am using it in the everyday meaning of idea or hypothesis, not the proper scientific meaning

scientific studies, as it surely cannot be possible for general practitioners to keep abreast of all advances in all fields of medicine. I bet there aren't many general practitioners that keep up to date with the progress of anxiety treatments, for example.

In a very controversial study in 2013 by a dozen doctors across the US who examined 363 articles about established practices in the New England Journal of Medicine from 2001 and 2010, it was determined that 146 of those studies suggested that current medical practices used by doctors across the country either had no benefit to the patient at all or were inferior to the practices they replaced. 138 of the studies showed the current practices were effective, and the remaining 79 were inconclusive[3].

Now as I say, I'm not telling you this to try and put down doctors (my brother would disown me), I'm telling you this just to demonstrate that many things that are done in medical practices around the World are out of date and not in line with the current scientific thinking. Doctors are more-often-than-not doing what they think is in your best interest, but occasionally they aren't in the best position to do this. This is another reason why a second opinion is always recommended when you see a doctor.

Okay, it's obvious, then, that I'm not a doctor, so what am I? Well in fact I was a physics teacher in Thailand for almost 20 years. Probably not what you were expecting but that is what I did. Now while I no longer do that and am currently working for a hotel in Vietnam, being "in the sciences", so to speak, for all those years gave me two things that were extremely useful for writing this

---

[3] A decade of reversal: an analysis of 146 contradicted medical practices – Prasad et. al. [2013]

book: A drive to find out why things are the way they are, and the skills to research those things properly without having to resort to certain "medical" websites.

So Why Did I Write THIS Book?

I think I've had this book brewing in me for a long time but without really knowing it. You see I suffered with anxiety for many years without realising what it was. Most of my issues were based in social anxiety and manifested themselves in different forms like telephone anxiety, public speaking anxiety, meeting new people anxiety, flying anxiety, small-talk anxiety, and toilet anxiety, but I have also had times when the world itself would fill me with dread. I would worry for hours about everything I said and did, and it was all I could do to keep the trembling inside my body in check. There were days when the anxious feelings were constant; I couldn't quite put my finger on it, but I was just continually on edge. These were the days that made me look for what was wrong with me. These were the days that led me to anxiety and GAD.

I have always been an introvert and am quite happy to stay at home alone and never contact another human for days on end, and to be honest, I have never wanted to change that. I have found, though, that some days are worse than others, and on these days, I have actively avoided people and social interaction of any kind even to the extent of skipping school lunches on occasion to avoid the canteen masses (although skipping the canteen food might not be an altogether bad idea).

On some days, I would be happy to talk to anyone, while others I would actively avoid people that I knew at the train station so as not to be locked into carriage small talk for the journey home. I didn't know why my anxiety flared up sometimes more than others I just knew it did. To be fair though, this wasn't enough for me to start thinking about writing a book. That had to wait until 2012 when I was diagnosed with IBS.

To cut a long and quite drawn-out story short, I had wrecked my gut through excessive antibiotic use in my younger years trying to battle my acne, and this had led to my IBS. It took me plenty of research to get to this conclusion, but it still wasn't what prompted me to write this book. That finally came when I started to notice a correlation between my IBS flare-ups and the episodes of anxiety that seemed to happen more and more often. It seemed that every time my anxiety levels were high, I was also bloated and nauseated from the IBS. This couldn't just be a coincidence, so I decided to research what the link could be. And to be fair, I really wasn't expecting the enormity of what I found.

This is the reason I wrote this book, as this book is the culmination of what I discovered. And what I discovered was astounding.

Anxiety

If you have ever suffered from any form of anxiety, you will know exactly what it is without me ever having to say a word. The overall feelings of anxiety are the same for most people. The severity of those feelings differs greatly.

Anxiety is generally the name given to the state of nervousness, fear, apprehension or worry that people feel, usually because they are about to do something or experience something that is unusual to them or involves a lot of pressure or uncertainty, or something they perceive could have a big impact on their life. This is normal anxiety and happens to everyone. We have all felt the knot in our stomachs and the sweaty palms before public speaking, or the dry mouth and sick feeling before a big exam. These are considered normal levels of anxiety, even though they offer no real benefit other than keeping your mind alert and can actually make things worse (imagine how much better you would be in an interview with no fear or anxiety).

The problems occur when people experience these feelings for the smallest of reason or even for no reasons at all. There are people that feel the symptoms of anxiety all the time. They feel the dread, the unease, and the apprehension, even when they are relaxing with no impending pressure situation. Others suffer anxiety at the slightest hint of social interaction or the thought of going to a busy place, and still others suffer through the constant gut-wrenching ruminations that something they have done is wrong and will cause a disaster.

There are many forms of anxiety, but the distinctions are mainly academic and lie primarily in what triggers the anxious moments. The basic nuts and bolts of each form of anxiety are pretty much the same, so it is important to know the basic mechanism of anxiety, how it works, and where it comes from, before we can even consider looking at beating it.

Where Does Anxiety Come From?

Anxiety, in fact, comes from a very necessary and ancient part of human survival and, in the past, has played a vital role in keeping us alive in the form of fear. Fear expresses itself in what is popularly known as the "Fight or Flight" response. Let's say for example, that you are wandering along one sunny day, and you come across a big hungry Grizzly Bear. Now I'm guessing that even if you have never set foot in bear country, you still have a fair sense that a hungry grizzly is not going to invite you for a polite spot of brunch; he's going to tear your head off. This knowledge is going to trigger a primeval reaction of self-preservation that we call "fear", and this natural surge in fear would prime your body in anticipation of having to fight or run away from that bear which could (although highly unlikely in the case of "fight", unless you're armed) save your life.

This was awesome in the old days of human history when everything we came across saw us as a two-legged entrée, but in today's world it is very unlikely that most of us will ever encounter a bear, or have-to run for our lives to keep ourselves off the menu, and although it is still possible to have life threatening situations, they are certainly less common or probable than they used to be. This does not mean that fear no longer exists though, on the contrary, it is possibly more prevalent than ever before. The problem is that in today's world fear often occurs with no real life-threatening trigger and it comes bundled with a side-serve of uncertainty, and when this happens, we call it **anxiety**.

You see, the fear response that our body activates when we experience fear is passed down to us from our ancestors, but the actual fears that we have are **learned**. In fact, when we first enter this world, we are born with only two natural fears – the fear of falling, and the fear of loud noises – fears that are necessary to keep us safe while we are babies.

The fear of loud noises can be seen in most animals, and even human babies, and is often known as the "Startle Pattern". Any loud noise will result in an automatic reaction of the eyes closing and the head ducking involuntarily. This is in-built in all of us and is as primitive a response as it gets.

All the other fears that we have, are learned from those around us as we are growing up or developed later within our environment. They are picked up without our realising it. Just as our young ancestors would have sensed the fear in their parents as a bear approached and learned to fear the bear, we have subliminally picked up on the fears and apprehensions of our parents and those around us.

The problem is of course that the fears that we have picked up are not the fears of wild animals, or marauding bands of thugs. They are not actually fears for our physical safety at all. They are fears for our social survival, fears for our future, fears for the safety of our inner well-being. This is why most people develop fears of situations that might test the safety of their social positioning or of their future success. They fear things like public speaking because they (unconsciously) worry that if they mess it up, they will let the people who trusted them down or look foolish in front of their peers and "go down in their estimations". They fear taking exams, or interviews, because they believe that the safety of their future success is riding on that single event. Of course, these fears are all blown out of proportion, but that's the point; that's what makes it anxiety.

Most people will recognise the sensation and feelings that they get through the worry or fear when they are about to do challenging things like public speaking or taking an exam. The fear and anxiety are remnants from those ancient times where bears and wolves were a real threat, and although we know an exam is not going to kill us, the fact that we feel weighed down by the importance of it can trigger the fight or flight response that will prime our body for a physical confrontation, a response that can be detrimental to our performance in the exam but can also ensure we put the required amount of effort and focus in to it.

This, of course, is normal anxiety that 99% of the world has experienced at some stage in their lives when something that they perceive to be life-affecting is about to happen. But what about anxiety disorders? What about panic disorders? What happens to those people that feel the weight of anxiety and fear throughout their waking days even when there is no exam, or town hall speech, or even a hungry grisly trying to eat them?

I think it is important to note first, that the anxiety suffered by a person with an anxiety disorder is basically the same as someone who only ever gets anxious before an important photo shoot; it is only the severity and the longevity that changes. If we were to plot the severity of the anxiety on a sliding scale, we would end up with regular folk at the one end, and the people who are diagnosed as suffering from anxiety disorders would be scattered everywhere else along the line. This is because the dividing line between normal and disordered is arbitrary, which basically means it was just decided upon by a group of psychiatrists in a room one day (literally). In fact, the line itself has been moved slightly over the years, as the main book of psychiatric diagnostics—the DSM—has been updated several times, and each time the diagnosis requirements are tweaked.

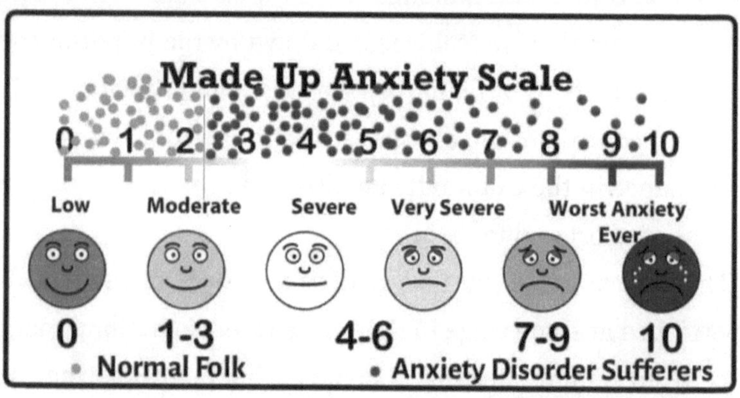

So, the question remains, what is it that makes the anxiety in some people much more severe and occur much more frequently than those who only experience anxiety when they are about to play lead guitar at the Riker's Island Christmas party? What makes these people so fearful about the things that are going to happen that it starts to impact their everyday lives? After all, there are people that live with an almost constant level of anxiety which means they are constantly apprehensive about what they are doing or what they are about to do, or they are worrying about what they have done or said.

To understand where the feelings and sensations from anxiety come from, we first need to understand the fear response.

The Fear response (Stress Response)

To see the origins of the fear response (or *stress response*) we need to go back to our analogy of confronting a bear in the woods. As soon as you see the bear the part of your brain called the *Hypothalamic-Pituitary-Adrenal* (HPA) *system*[4] is automatically activated to prepare you for a fight or to run away. This is a response that has evolved in us over millions of years, as the caveman who could fight the hardest or run the fastest would be more likely to survive and have children. This means, then, that when the fight or flight response is triggered, it is for the sole purpose of making us better fighting or running machines.

For this aim, the HPA starts by releasing steroid hormones like cortisol into the body which play an integral part in the organisation of the human body systems and priming them for battle (or running away) and acts like an early warning alarm system. It also releases important neurotransmitters, like adrenaline, that activate a fear response in the *amygdala* and set the rest of the body into action resulting in improved alertness and

---

4 The role of the hypothalamic-pituitary-adrenal axis in neuroendocrine responses to stress | Smith, vale [2006]

muscle strength. It is these initial chemicals that cause the sensations of fear and the sense of dread that characterise anxiety.

Once the neurotransmitters have gone to work, they kick-start the rest of the body's systems into action and prepare them for what's coming. First, the heart rate and blood pressure increase automatically, the breathing becomes rapid, and the spleen ramps up its output of red and white blood cells, all to get as much oxygen as it can quickly to the limbs. The more oxygen in the cells, the more energy you've got ready for the short power bursts you might need to fight a crazed polar bear. This also gives rise to the pounding chest, shallow breathing, and shaking limbs that many anxiety sufferers experience.

As the fear response heightens, fluid is taken from nonessential locations, such as the mouth, resulting in dryness and throat spasms which can cause difficulty swallowing. The skin is also affected, as blood is moved away from the skin's surface in case of damage leaving a feeling of cool clamminess and sweaty palms.

These are the results of the fight or flight response, and they are excellent for preparing our fragile human bodies to fight like Tyson or run like Bolt when stalked by a pack of ne'er-do-well wolves, but unfortunately it means they also become the symptoms of anxiety when there is not a wolf in sight. I am sure you recognise some of these symptoms from your own experiences. They are simply the symptoms of the fight or flight response and can never harm you directly, as they are built in for your survival, but for people with anxiety disorders, when these symptoms become an everyday aspect of life, they can be devastating.

Panic Attacks

If you were reading the symptoms above and recognised that you have experienced them yourself in an extreme and unbearable fashion, that made you feel like you were about to die, but there was no "angry badger" to trigger them, then you have likely suffered a panic attack. A panic attack is basically an intense and full-on fear response with all the same physical and mental symptoms associated with the fight or flight response to a life-threatening experience but with the absence of any real trigger. It can just happen randomly and without warning. What makes the panic attack worse and can leave you in a vicious cycle are the effects that anxiety can have on your memory.

Effects on memory

One of the most surprising effects that our hypothetical bear could have on the body is to the memory: The initial release of the neurotransmitters suppresses certain activity at the front of the brain that is related to **short-term memory**, inhibition, and rational thought. This allows the body to jump straight into survival mode without waiting to sit and think it through logically, which would probably result in being fatally groped by the bear.

Unfortunately, today where bears are few and far between in most people's lives, these memory effects are usually more problematic than helpful. For example, the short-term memory effect can prevent people who are suffering from panic or anxiety attacks from observing the attack with a rational mind. The brain is hard-wired to leap into survival mode and so it can be difficult to rationalise the issue at hand and so hard to "calm yourself down". It also makes the fear response less helpful with the "modern-day triggers" like public speaking or exam taking.

The biggest problem, however, is the long-term memory effects. If a caveman happened to be assaulted by a cheesed-off grizzly and survived, then the memory of the attack would be stored in the long-term memory, so if he ever ran into a bear again, the memory would resurface, and he would know to look at how cheesed-off the bear was in the future. This could be lifesaving if he lived in a place that was particularly disgruntling for bears. However, it is not always as useful in today's world: When an anxiety sufferer experiences a panic or anxiety attack, the reason for the attack is locked away in the long-term memory as well, to be used again in the future for "protection". The problem is of course that anxiety usually doesn't have definable triggers, so what the brain remembers is just the place or situation where the episode occurred. This means that each time the sufferer returns to that place or situation again, the brain could instigate another "fight or flight" anxiety attack because the brain now views it as a threat.

With panic attacks, it is often the actual panic attack itself that becomes the threat, so when people return to a situation or place where they have previously experienced an attack, the brain's instigation of a fear response, linked to the memory, will also lead to a new fear in the sufferer—the fear of having a panic attack. This results in a cycle of fear which inevitably results in another panic attack. This leads the person into the world of panic disorders

What are Panic Disorders?

Panic disorder is the name given to describe people who are stuck in this cycle of fear. A person that is suffering from anxiety can have a panic attack at any time without any cause, but they are usually random and relatively rare. If, however, the brain has committed a place, event, or situation as a panic attack trigger to the long-term memory and a person becomes scared of visiting these places or repeating the situation for fear of a recurrence of the panic attack, then this person has a panic disorder.

The fear, of course, gets worse over time. The person's fear of having another panic attack feeds the already saved memory of the "threat" which in turn increases the likelihood of having an attack. Panic disorders are self-fulfilling fears that will only worsen over time.

The Anxiety Cycle

Even if you don't suffer from panic disorders, this effect on memory will be playing a major part in keeping your anxiety from stopping on its own. Each time your body endures a fear response, even if it is relatively mild, the brain will be locking away what it considers the trigger to be (the situation, place, or event) in its long-term memory. This creates a cycle whereby negative anxious thoughts and memories trigger a fear response with physical symptoms which creates new (or adds to existing) memories, which generates more negative anxious thoughts, and so on.

It is easier to see if we simplify it and show how the chemicals play their role: Anxious negative thoughts trigger the fear response which releases adrenaline and cortisol into the body, and the release of these chemicals puts our minds into high alert and self-preservation mode which naturally makes our thoughts negative. It is a vicious cycle that normally continues until the danger has passed and we are safe. Unfortunately, as anxiety has no real danger and often no perceivable threat, the cycle can continue for much longer than it is meant to.

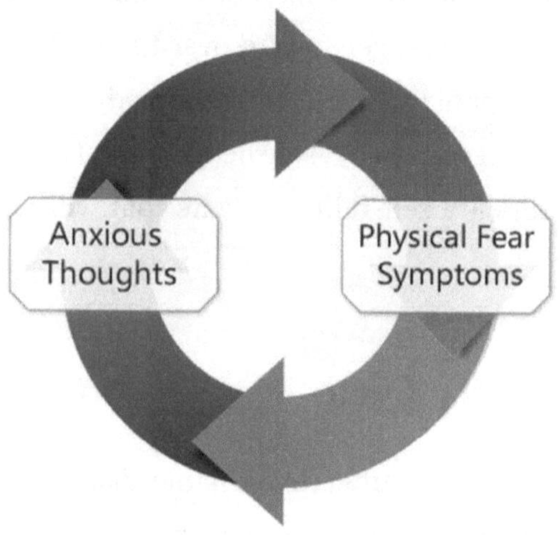

The question is, though, much like the age-old chicken and the egg problem, which comes first the negative anxious thoughts or the physical fear symptoms? Most people automatically presume that their anxious thoughts are the original culprit, cranking out the fear response symptoms that they are so well acquainted with, and very often they are. But what if something else was creating the symptoms? What if the adrenaline and cortisol had different triggers and the anxious thoughts were created (or at least worsened) by this atmosphere of constant fear?

That is what we are going to look at here. We are going to look at the root cause of this heightened anxiety and why so many people are stuck in the cycle with no way out.

The question we are going to ask is this: What is it that starts the anxiety cycle turning when there are seemingly no rational triggers present? This is the question that I am hoping to answer for you throughout this book.

Is There More Anxiety Now Than in History?

It is certainly not easy to determine the change in rates of anxiety over the years, as there are several factors involved in comparing anxiety rates over generations. Not least of all is the stigma attached to all kinds of mental illnesses in the past that prevented people from ever admitting to suffering from such. That said though, it is widely considered that, with around 40 million people suffering from some form of anxiety in the US even before covid, these rates were the highest they had ever been, and it now seems to be even higher in the post-covid world. And it's not just the US: Between 1997 and 2009 the UK saw a rise of 12.8% in anxiety related illnesses. A rise of 12.8 % in 13 years gives us a rough idea of how anxiety has rapidly become one of the biggest healthcare problems of the 21st century, and it is clear now that covid has only made things worse. In fact, one study estimates that there were about 298 million anxiety disorder sufferers in the world in 2020, and an extra 76.2 million more were added solely because of covid and the associated lockdowns[5].

---

[5] Global prevalence and burden of depressive and anxiety disorders in 204 countries and territories in 2020 due to the COVID-19 pandemic | Santomauro et al. [2021]

Now, without a doubt, some of the pre-covid rise was due to the change in cultural and political climate over the past half-century. The threat of nuclear annihilation, and the cold war, created an atmosphere of anxiety throughout the world which governments and media subsequently took advantage of and built upon for their own ends to the extent of actually propagating fear and anxiety to gain control or coverage. This same mechanism certainly holds some blame for the rise in cases due to covid as well.

But there has been another major change in the western world over the past few decades, and I believe that the research included in this book goes someway to explaining how these changes have helped lead to the meteoric rise of anxiety in the world today.

Do Cases of Anxiety Differ Around the World?

While there is not a huge difference, and what difference there is seems to be closing, anxiety cases in different regions of the world do seem to differ with the numbers of anxiety cases in the west being still somewhat higher than the anxiety cases in the east. If we look at the results of the *National Comorbidity Survey* on the 12 month counts of people with **social anxiety disorder**, we see that for adults in the US the figure is around 7.1% - 7.9%. In contrast, the numbers for adults in East Asian countries seem to be much lower with Korea being only 0.2% - 0.6% and Japan being only 0.8%. Even if we count all anxiety disorders, the US was at 6.3% of the total population in 2015, while Japan was only 3.3%. Now it is true that this could be due to a stigmatism in the east with what is thought of as a mental illness and therefore reduces the number of admitted sufferers, but with the rise in stress management in countries like Japan, I would doubt that this plays as big a role as it used to. I would also hazard a guess that the stigmatism is just as great if not greater in the UK and other European countries right now anyway.

If this is the case, and we can presume that the anxiety statistics from all countries are as reliable as each other, then we must ask the question why does the West have significantly more social anxiety sufferers than the East and higher anxiety disorder sufferers in general? Some of the differences will be down to social pressures and the way government and media have evolved in the West. There is certainly a case for saying that the capitalistic viewpoint of individualism in the western world creates an ideal breeding ground for anxiety when compared to the more social and community driven communities in the Eastern World, but is it enough to count for the marked differences in all kinds of anxiety disorders between the regions?

My hope is that this book will go some way to identifying a different cause of this anxiety and give some possible answers as to why different regions have different levels of anxiety. I also hope that I can give you enough information and advice that you will be able to go away from this book and tackle your anxiety yourself without the need for medication.

So, let's start at the beginning.

The Beginning

As you might have already guessed, the theme of this book is the idea that it is *physical* processes in the body that start the anxiety cycle turning and keep the levels of fight or flight chemicals high within the brain, and these physical processes are caused, or at least worsened, by the foods we eat, beverages we drink, and medicines we put in our body, and are a major cause of anxiety in the world today.

Now this is not a new idea. For years, you may have been told that drinking coffee or alcohol was bad for anxiety, or that drinking green tea was good. Everywhere you look today, someone is singling out a specific food that you should or shouldn't eat if you have anxiety.

What I wanted to do was pull all this together and find a single root cause of how food and drink are causing our anxiety and what overall food types we should and shouldn't eat to prevent anxiety from ever happening again. The important part for me was not the foods themselves but the mechanisms they used to trigger anxiety. Once you know how it works, the rest is easy. Of course, with the body being so complex, there are many ways that drugs like caffeine might stimulate anxiety, but I wanted to distil the idea down to a general mechanism by which a lifestyle or diet might lead to overriding anxiety. The simplest question to start off with, then, was "has anyone ever checked to see if an overall diet can trigger anxiety?"

Can the Food We Eat Cause Anxiety?

Before we begin getting into details at all, and even think about looking at reasons why, we need to know if the foods we eat, and the diets we follow, have any bearing on our anxiety at all. To answer this for us, a group of researchers took a random sample of 1046 women aged 20 – 93 from the population and compared their overall diets to their general mental state by using a standardized questionnaire and interview[6].

After adjustments for age, socioeconomic status, education, and health behaviours were made, it was found that a "traditional" diet of vegetables, fruit, meat, fish, and whole grains was associated with *lower odds* for anxiety disorders than a "western" diet of processed and fried foods, refined grains, sugary products, and beer. This basically means that what is generally considered to be a "healthier" diet resulted in fewer cases of anxiety disorders and an overall better mental health when compared to the more "fast food" style diet. Now this might not be surprising to you, but it does at least give us an idea that healthy food might not only lead to a healthy body, but also a healthier mind—a mind with less chance of anxiety.

This is certainly not the only study to show a relationship between anxiety and food, but it was a nice simple one to kick us off. Now while this simple study certainly does not prove that diet *causes* anxiety, it does demonstrate at least some correlation between the two, and this is certainly enough to grab our interest

---

[6] Association of Western and traditional diets with depression and anxiety in women |Jacka, Pasco et al [2010]

to investigate further. So, if there is a correlation between diet and anxiety, the next question to ask is why? Or better still, how?

Introducing the Gut

If you didn't already know, the gut, otherwise known as the **gastrointestinal tract,** is the hugely long tube that travels from your mouth to your anus. If you think about it (and I bet you haven't), you could even say that the contents of your gut are not strictly inside of you. The very fact that your gut runs all the way through you with both ends open to the world means that the contents of the gut are never truly inside you at all, much like the hole of a doughnut isn't really inside the doughnut. But that's the whole point, the gut is there to keep bad things from getting inside your body and into your blood.

When you eat, the food is taken in through the mouth and is immediately set upon by enzymes that begin to break the food down into more useable forms. This continues as the food moves through the stomach and the small intestines—enzymes and bacteria do their work on the food, breaking it down into something we can use. This is called digestion.

The good stuff is then allowed to move through the walls of the small intestine into our body for our energy and nutritional needs, while what is literally called "waste" is pushed through the large intestine, relieved of water, and pooped out of the anus. This is traditionally what the sole purpose and role of the gut was. It was for all intents and purposes a tube that took everything we need out of our food and got rid of the rest. That was it.

Can the Gut Do More Than Just Digest?

This is the question that we need to start with: Is the gut responsible for more than just digesting our food? Well let's first look at our own experiences. I am sure you have experienced a "gut wrenching experience" or had "butterflies in your stomach" during some stressful or nerve-wracking event. Severe stress can even send some people running to the toilet. Most people would agree that stressful or fearful situations can certainly be felt in the stomach, and so we can presume that there must be some link between the brain and the gut that deals with more than just automatic digestion.

It has indeed been found that the brain and the gut are actually linked more than we initially thought, and the gastrointestinal tract is sensitive to emotional stress of all kinds from signals sent to it from the brain: Anger, sadness, stress, fear, anxiety—any of these emotions, and many more, can trigger an effect in the gut. This has been found to be thanks to the **vagus nerve**, the 10th cranial nerve, that runs all the way from the brain stem to the gut and carries the signals that result in that "churning of the stomach" when anxious.

So, the gut can turn mental episodes into real physical distress. Now that wouldn't really be shocking to most people, but it might be more impressive if it could do the reverse.

Can the Gut Affect Our Mind?

If the vagus nerve stretches from the brain to the gut, it seems only logical that signals should be able to be sent both ways. If signals can be sent from the brain to the gut, then surely, they should also be sent from the gut to the brain.

Well scientists have proven that not only can signals be sent from the gut to the brain, but a whole lot more signals are sent from the gut to the brain than from the brain to the gut. In fact, a whopping 90% of the fibres in the vagus nerve carry information from the gut to the brain and only 10% for the other way around. This gives us an insight into just how powerful the gut is and how misunderstood it has been for the past century. If significantly more signals are sent from the gut to the brain, then it suggests that not only does the gut look after itself, but it also affects many other aspects of our lives and health.

I guess the question is, can it really affect our mood? Well, the answer is a resounding yes and in an astonishing number of ways: The vagus nerve first became of interest in the 19th century when doctors noted that they could suppress seizures simply by applying pressure to the nerve, thus demonstrating its effect on the brain. A more recent study saw researchers cut the vagus nerve in mice so that signals could only travel from the brain to the gut but not the other way round[7]. The results showed that the mice with the altered vagus demonstrated lower levels of fear but seemed to retain that fear for much longer.

This research showed that the vagus nerve carries signals of "gut instinct" to the brain which will have a significant impact on how the brain responds to fear.

---

[7] Gut Vagal Afferents Differentially Modulate Innate Anxiety and Learned Fear | Klarer et al. [2014]

The Gut as the Second Brain

It certainly appears then that the gut might play a role in at least some of our feelings of fear, but it is only very recently that researchers are beginning to realise just how big a role it plays. Unlike the dumb digestive tube that we were dealing with a decade ago, the gut has revealed itself to be something far more impressive.

In its roughly 9m length from oesophagus to anus, the gut has an estimated 100 million neurons embedded in its walls. These neurons are the exact same nerve cells that make up the brain and are the cells responsible for the brain being able to do what it does. Now, while 100 million is nowhere near the number that inhabits the human brain (closer to 100 billion), it is significantly more than can be found in the brain and entire nervous system of a frog or a mouse.

This is why many people now refer to the gut as the "second brain" and why it has now been named the ***Enteric Nervous System.*** It doesn't stop there though, the gut also uses neurotransmitters (chemical messengers) like serotonin, just like the brain does, and creates its own individual neurotransmitters that are not made anywhere else. Overall, the gut uses or produces around 30 different neurotransmitters (which is on a par with the brain) and, in fact, over 90% of the body's serotonin is created there.

There is just no question that the gut is much more than the simple digestive tube that we have thought it to be over the past few decades.

The Link between Gut and Mental Disorders

To be fair, a link between the gut and mental disorders is not a new idea. It has in fact been around for centuries. Hippocrates, the father of medicine who lived in Greece between 460 and 370 BC said, *"All diseases begin in the gut"*. Even Philippe Pinel who is widely considered the father of modern psychiatry believed that mental illnesses began as physical problems in the gut, saying *"The primary seat of insanity lies generally in the region of the stomach and intestines"*, and this was in the 18th century.

In 1930 two doctors, named John Stokes and Donald Pillsbury, called the gut-brain connection the "unifying theory" as they believed problems with the gut accounted for the link between emotional disorders and inflammatory skin conditions.

Unfortunately, these ideas were not widely accepted by mainstream medicine, and instead, psychiatry started on the path of separating the mind and body that we still find ourselves on today.

In fact, it is only in the last few years that medicine has stopped scoffing at these remarks and been forced to take them a little more seriously, as study after study seems to show that Hippocrates and Pinel might have been right all along. Sadly, much of the medical community still does not believe such a link exists in any meaningful form. In fact, as recently as 2002, the ideas of Stokes and Pillsbury were called nonsense at an annual dermatology meeting.

Thankfully that didn't stop researchers from studying the relationship between gut disorders and mental illnesses, and, when they did, they found that people with gastrointestinal issues often suffered from depression or anxiety disorders also.

One study showed that between 70% and 90% of people with IBS (irritable bowel syndrome) had also demonstrated psychological issues[8]. The same study also showed that 27% of people already diagnosed with major depression displayed symptoms fitting the criteria for IBS while only 2.5% of the control group did. Other studies have shown that up to 46% of patients with panic disorder also displayed symptoms matching the criteria for IBS[9].

While these studies do not make it clear whether the gastrointestinal disorders caused the mental illnesses or vice versa, there is certainly a strong link between the two, and if we look at a different study showing that people with coeliac disease (gluten intolerance) also displayed a high prevalence of panic disorders[10], it seems at least possible that gastrointestinal disorders do affect mental state.

It is also equally likely (if not more so in my opinion) that both the gastrointestinal distress and the mental disorder are caused by a common origin, such as *inflammation*. I will discuss inflammation in the Leaky Gut section as I feel this is one of the likeliest causes of both gastrointestinal issues and anxiety disorders.

---

[8] Major depression and irritable bowel syndrome: is there a relationship? | Masand, Kaplan et al. [1995]

[9] Comorbidity of irritable bowel syndrome in psychiatric patients: a review | Garakani et al [2003]

[10] Association between panic disorder, major depressive disorder and celiac disease: A possible role of thyroid autoimmunity | Carta, Hardoy et al [2002]

It is clear, though, that the gut is a lot more powerful than we originally gave it credit for, and while it cannot do any cognitive "thinking" it could be playing a much larger role in our overall mental and emotional wellbeing than we initially thought.

How Does Our Gut Send Signals That Trigger Anxiety?

We can see, then, that our gut and brains are inter-linked, and I already knew through my own personal experience that somehow my gut was sending a signal to my brain that triggered heightened anxiety, or at least something was triggering both my IBS and my anxiety at the same time. The next step seemed to be to find out how the gut could trigger anxiety or what there could be that might be affecting both my gut and anxiety at the same time. What I found basically boiled down to two things:

1. Microbiota

The bacteria and other microorganisms that live in the digestive tracts (guts) of animals, sometimes called the gut flora.

2. Leaky Gut

A permeability of the membrane in the gut that can allow partially digested food and gut bacteria to enter the body leading to an immune response.

These two things are closely linked to each other and usually act in tandem, but sometimes they can cause problems separately which is why I will address them as such.

Microbiota - Bacteria in the Gut

The gut is home to a whole ecosystem of bacteria and fungi—some good and some bad. In fact, there is somewhere in the region of 100 trillion microorganisms that live throughout your gut[11], which is about 10 times more than all the other cells in your body put together. To put this number in perspective, it is over 10,000 times more than all the people on the planet, and if you think about it, this means, that in number alone, your body is more bacteria than human. There are so many of them that the whole ecosystem of bacteria in your gut weighs a staggering 3 pounds. That's about the same as your brain.

Not only are they large in number, but they are also incredibly diverse genetically. Scientists have so far identified about ten thousand different species of gut bacteria with a vast range of genetic codes. You may remember when scientists finally cracked the code of mapping the human genome, they discovered that humans have about twenty-two thousand genes. Well, that pales into comparison to the more than three *million* genes that are present in the bacteria that live within us.

In fact, there are so many kinds of bacteria that call the gut home, with so many different genes, that the combination of bacteria that live within your gut will be completely different to the ones that live within mine. They are like a fingerprint and no two people will have exactly the same mix.

---

[11] Role of the gut microbiota in health and chronic gastrointestinal disease: understanding a hidden metabolic organ | Guinane, Cotter [2013]

These microorganisms that live in your gut are often called the **microbiota**, and they make up an ecosystem that scientists call the human **microbiome**. It is only very recently that scientists are beginning to understand how important these little organisms are to our overall health.

Now it is important to know, that these ten thousand or so species of microorganism that can inhabit your body are all completely different and will do different things to the gut. Some of them are good, friendly bacteria (commensal bacteria), and some of them are not so good, and certainly not so friendly (pathogens).

In a healthy gut, the good bacteria keep the bad in check and go about their daily grind unnoticed, performing important jobs such as aiding with digestion; absorption of food; breaking down of proteins, fibre, fat, and carbohydrates; the production of substances to transport vitamins and minerals around the body; the breaking down of bile; and the regulation of neurotransmitters.

Another of their jobs that is slowly being investigated is their importance in controlling and regulating the immune system: The gut hosts most of the Lymphoid tissue in the body, meaning that about 70% of the entire immune system is to be found in the gut, giving ever increasing importance to our small bacterial friends.

We are still learning the full extent of the role these little critters play in our body's everyday functions, but it is slowly becoming apparent that it is greater than we ever imagined.

Can Gut Bacteria Affect Mental State?

We have already seen that there is a link between gut health and mental health, and so the next logical step is to see if the microbiota in the gut also plays a part in this gut-brain axis.

Its importance comes into play when we remember that everybody's microbiota is different. Like fingerprints, the microbiota in the gut is unique to each person, and it is these slight variations—changes in diversity or good/bad bacteria ratios—that could possibly lead to health problems elsewhere in the body. There have been many studies that have shown how the microbiota affect mood and mental state, and while the research is still in its infancy, with most of the studies being performed on mice, there have been a few interesting results:

One of the most interesting studies done on mice took some healthy adults and compared a normal control group with a group that had had its gut flora (microbiota) removed with antibiotics[12]. The mice that had no gut bacteria demonstrated changes in behaviour, such as becoming less cautious or anxious when compared to their normal counterparts and were found to have increased levels of *brain-derived neurotrophic factor (BDNF),* which has been shown to be reduced in people with anxiety disorders. When the antibiotics were stopped, the gut microbiota returned to normal along with the mice's behaviour.

---

[12] Gut bacteria linked to behavior: That anxiety may be in your gut, not in your head. https://www.sciencedaily.com/releases/2011/05/110517110315.htm

To take it one step further, and to confirm that the effect was due to the bacteria in the gut, the researchers then transplanted the bacteria from one set of normal mice into bacteria-free mice that were genetically prone to a different behaviour pattern. They found that when they transferred bacteria from mice which were genetically prone to being adventurous into bacteria-free mice that were prone to be passive, the recipient of the bacteria suddenly became more active and daring. The same thing also occurred when the passive and adventurous mice roles were reversed. This shows us that even when we consider a behaviour to be "genetically predisposed" the microbiota play an important role in the realisation of that behaviour.

Microbiota were also shown to play a role in anxiety when researchers measured the separation anxiety of normal mice and bacteria-free mice when taken from their mothers[13]: The regular mice experienced separation anxiety while the bacteria-free mice did not. It seems, then, that the microbiota (in mice at least) plays some part in regulating fear and anxiety in the brain.

How about in Humans?

Although mice are often a very good analogue for humans, thanks to over 95% of their genome being the same as ours along with similar biological and behavioural characteristics, it is not always 100% certain that what happens in a mouse will happen in a human. Therefore, it is important to look at results in humans as well. There are a growing number of studies being done on humans

---

[13] Postnatal microbial colonization programs the hypothalamic–pituitary–adrenal system for stress response in mice | Sudo et al. [2004]

to test the relationship between the microbiota and brain function—some of which are quite interesting. Some interesting results have also been obtained completely by accident:

One such group of researchers was testing an idea that injecting human patients, who had cancer, with a certain bacterium would stimulate their immune system into attacking the cancer and therefore curing it. What they found, though, was that although there was no effect on the cancer, the patients all experienced a huge improvement in their mood and the quality of their life[14].

One scientist stated:

"It was supposed to be a double-blind study, but the investigators could nearly always tell who was on the genuine treatment because their whole attitude, their demeanour, changed"

It seems then that changing the make-up of the gut microbiota can indeed have a significant impact on mental state and mood. The question is of course, are there certain bacteria that affect anxiety more than others? Well, it certainly seems that there are specific bacteria that can be added to the gut which can either reduce or increase anxiety, and there appear to be more and more researchers testing this and finding the results consistent. Healthy bacteria that are added to a person's gut to positively affect the gut microbiota are called **probiotics**.

In one study, healthy people were given a mixture of probiotics containing Lactobacillus helveticus and B. longum, or a placebo,

---

[14]http://www.newscientist.com/article/dn19951-infectious-moods-the-happiness-injection.html

for 30 days[15]. They were then evaluated using questionnaires to check anxiety, depression, and stress. The probiotic group demonstrated significantly lower psychological distress than the control group.

In another study, 39 patients with chronic fatigue syndrome were randomly chosen to receive either 24 billion units of Lactobacillus casei, or a placebo, for two months. After this time, the patients provided stool samples and completed anxiety questionnaires. The researchers found a significant rise in Lactobacillus and Bifidobacteria in the stool samples of those taking the probiotic and a marked decrease in anxiety symptoms when compared to the control group[16].

In yet another study in 2013, researchers at UCLA took a sample of healthy women and asked them to drink a beverage with four strains of probiotics added twice a day for four weeks. Once the four weeks were up, the women's brains were scanned as they were shown photos of either angry or sad faces and asked to match them with faces of similar emotion. The women that had consumed the probiotics showed much lower brain activity in the areas of the brain responsible for sensory and emotional behaviour when compared to the women who did not have the drink making them less prone to anxious responses[17].

In a more recent study, researchers at William & Mary and the University of Maryland tested how fermented foods affected the

---

[15] Beneficial psychological effects of a probiotic formulation (Lactobacillus helveticus R0052 and Bifidobacterium longum R0175) in healthy human volunteers | Messaoudi et al. [2011]

[16] A randomized, double-blind, placebo-controlled pilot study of a probiotic in emotional symptoms of chronic fatigue syndrome | Rao, Bested et. al. [2009]

[17] https://newsroom.ucla.edu/releases/changing-gut-bacteria-through-245617

anxiety in young adults. What they discovered was that the probiotics in fermented foods, when taken regularly, decreased the levels of anxiety in the subjects[11a]. This study was building on previous animal studies where they had found that probiotics given regularly to animals increased the levels of GABA production in the brain of those animals, which reduced their anxiety.

On the flipside, an alternative study was done whereby mice were given the pathogenic bacteria C.jejuni, and, after only two days, the mice were noted to display significantly more anxiety-like behaviour than before the bacteria's introduction[18].

There are certainly many more studies like these that show, quite clearly, that in both mice and humans there are some bacteria that have positive effects on anxiety and other bacteria that have negative effects on anxiety[19], and these studies have become increasingly popular and convincing over the past ten years. These bacteria can be found naturally in the microbiota of the body, and usually the balance and diversity of the microbiota is such that anxiety is kept at a necessary level to keep us "safe from danger". After all, some fear is a good thing.

Occasionally though, these levels will be changed, and the diversity of the microbiota decreased which can then give rise to a greater number of pathogenic bacteria. As we have seen, this can adversely affect our anxiety levels either by sending their

---

[18] Campylobacter jejuni infection increases anxiety-like behavior in the holeboard: possible anatomical substrates for viscerosensory modulation of exploratory behavior | Goehler et. al. [2008]

[19] Gut microbiota in anxiety and depression: Pathogenesis and therapeutics | Bibbo et. al., (2022)

The gut microbiome in social anxiety disorder: evidence of altered composition and function | Butler et. al., (2023)

neurotransmitters to receptors in the vagus nerve, triggering an anxiety response from the brain, instigating an immune response, or leading to a leaky gut, which I will talk about in the next chapter.

How Can the Microbiota be Changed?

It is important to note that each of us develops in the womb with a gut that is completely free of all bacteria and fungi, but as soon as we are born, our guts begin to be invaded from the world around us. The first major colonisation of bacteria comes from our mother's birth canal during a natural birth and then through the mother's milk. It is interesting to note that this time also coincides with the development of the stress-response system. After this initial colonisation, more diverse colonies are produced from the environment.

It has been found in several studies[20], that although there is a genetic component that determines which bacteria will thrive in a gut, the environment plays a crucial role as only those bacteria in the immediate environment can colonise.

This was demonstrated when researchers took a bacteria-free mouse and placed it in the same living environment as a normal mouse. After some time, the bacteria free mouse was found to have the same bacterial diversity in its gut as the normal mouse.

This shows that your gut microbiota can be affected by the environment and the people you interact with. In fact, the simple

---

[20] A cross-sectional study of gut microbiota composition in rural and urban Chinese adults | Li, J., Zhang, J., Wang, Y., Wang, L., Zhang, C., & Zhang, L. (2019)

act of moving-house, or moving to a different state or country, can radically change your gut microbiota[21].

This is taken a step further with the "hygiene hypothesis" that suggests that in countries with high levels of hygiene, such as in the industrialised west, the gut microbiota in many of the people is underdeveloped as the environment contains insufficient bacteria to create a healthy and complete microbiome.[22]

Diet

As you might expect, the food you eat can also seriously change your microbiota. Eat the wrong foods and you could be feeding the wrong kind of bacteria. I will talk more about the right and wrong kinds of foods for maintaining a healthy and diverse microbiota later, but you should know that changes in microbiota due to diet can happen quickly and radically.

One study to demonstrate this was done by the universities of Harvard and Duke with eleven volunteers, who, for five days, restricted their diet to meals made with rice, tomato, squash, peas, garlic, lentils, banana, mango and papaya. They then returned to their regular balanced diets for a week.

Finally, they spent another five days eating only fatty meats, eggs and cheese. By analysing the composition of the microbiota in each subject, they saw that after only three days of changing the diet each time, there was significant variation to the activity and

---

[21] Variation in the Gut Microbiota of Laboratory Mice Is Related to Both Genetic and Environmental Factors | Hufeldt et. al. [2010]

[22] Gut Reaction: Environmental Effects on the Human Microbiota | Phillips [2009]

composition of the bacteria. This study is eye-opening as it shows us exactly how quickly the composition of microbiota can change[23].

A bad diet of processed foods, and too much sugar and processed carbohydrates, can unbalance your microbiota. Certain unfriendly bacteria and yeasts thrive on these processed sugars and carbohydrates which can result in them out-growing the good bacteria and taking over the gut. Unfortunately, these foods are what are considered the staples of a western diet by many people today.

Antibiotics

Antibiotics are used to kill bacteria; that is what they do, and they do it well. The problem is that they don't just kill bad bacteria, they kill all the bacteria, good and bad, that reside in your gut. Now while this may sound fine, as at least there will be no unhealthy bacteria (and the bacteria-free mice seemed to do well for themselves), the problem is that it can take between 4 to 6 weeks for a fully diverse and healthy gut flora to "grow back", and in this time, dangerous opportunistic fungi and yeasts can colonise and take over.

Remember yeasts and fungi are not affected by antibiotics and without the good bacteria to keep them in check, extended periods of time on antibiotics can result in the colonisation of some quite nasty candida (yeast) strains. This is basically what happened to me.

---

[23] Diet rapidly and reproducibly alters the human gut microbiome | David et.al [2013]

It should also be noted that using the terms "good" and "bad" bacteria, or "healthy" and "unhealthy" bacteria, are oversimplifications. Many of these so called "unhealthy" bacteria are still essential parts of the microbiome, as they have also evolved in our guts and often have important roles to play. We have already noted, for example, that some anxiety is essential for our survival, and many of these bacteria provide that level of anxiety. What we don't want is for these bacteria to overpopulate the gut and crowd out the anxiety-*reducing* bacteria which would result in an unnaturally high level of anxiety—the very situation we are looking to eliminate.

Probiotics

As mentioned earlier, probiotics are good bacteria that can be artificially added to the gut to build up the number and diversity of beneficial bacteria to get an overall healthier microbiota.

I will discuss probiotics later, as they are an essential part of tackling anxiety through diet and a change in microbiota.

Stress

One of the important ways in which the microbiota in the gut can be altered is through stress. Researchers have shown that mice that have been put through a stressor test have significantly different gut microbiota to mice that were not subjected to the test[24]. This has been shown to be true in human trials in recent years also[25].

As stress is a broad term and certainly can encompass anxiety and fear within it, this gives rise to the possibility of a feedback loop, or vicious cycle, as the microbiota can, either directly or indirectly, cause anxiety, and in return the anxiety will cause further change in the microbiota through the fear response. Unless manually halted, this vicious cycle could continue forever with worsening effects.

It also gives rise to a possible physical reaction to traumatic events. This means that as well as disturbing life-events causing Post Traumatic Stress Disorder (PTSD) in the mind, it will drastically change the microbiota in the gut which could lead to permanent changes to mental wellbeing until the microbiota is rebalanced.

[24] Exposure to a social stressor alters the structure of the intestinal microbiota: implications for stressor-induced immunomodulation | Bailey et. al [2011]

[25] Effects of psychological, environmental and physical stress on the gut microbiota: a systematic review and meta-analysis | Galley, J. M., & Bailey, M. T. (2021)

Leaky Gut and Immune Response

Another consequence of an overgrowth of bad bacteria and another major cause of anxiety is what is commonly named "Leaky Gut". Its proper name is **Intestinal Permeability** and, as the name suggests, is when the lining of the gut becomes perforated and begins to allow larger molecules, like partially undigested foods and microbiota, through into the blood supply. When this happens, it is possible for the immune system to target these unknown invaders as though they were pathogens and treat them like they would with any dangerous foreign body—by triggering a systemic *inflammation.*

Inflammation is the name given to the biological response when our immune system is called into action following some damage to the body. I am sure you have experienced the symptoms of normal inflammation due to trauma, like cuts, scratches, or bruises, and infections—heat, redness, pain, and swelling. This is the immune system kicking into action and triggering inflammation at the damaged area to heal it as fast as possible.

The problem with leaky gut is that the material that slips through the net into the bloodstream triggers an inflammation response that is not normal. Instead of inflammation being localised at an injured spot on the body, the inflammation due to leaky gut is systemic and can reach the brain. This is like when the body is invaded by the common cold or flu viruses: The immune system goes into full inflammation mode to destroy the invading virus resulting in the sick feeling that people usually associate with the flu or a cold. It is the inflammation that causes the sickness not the virus itself.

The inflammation caused by leaky gut, then, can have a similar impact on the body, and the production of its associated "invader fighting" cells (cytokines), and their chemicals, can result in anxiety symptoms as they pass through the blood-brain barrier and reach the HPA in the brain.

In fact, research, done by scientists at the University of Virginia School of Medicine, showed that the brain is *directly* connected to the immune system through vessels that were previously not known to exist[26]. This means that science is finding new and easier pathways for the gut to influence the brain through the immune response and inflammation.

It is this inflammation of the brain that is a major cause of anxiety in many people, but its origins are in the gut. Just think back to the last time you had a cold and think how good your mood was.

Several studies have been done that show a relationship between anxiety disorders and certain inflammation markers in the blood[27]. There are a few main culprits that have been studied:

LPS

One of the most common anxiety-inducing inflammations is when there is an immune response to the chemical

---

[26] Missing link found between brain, immune system; major disease implications | Kipnis [2015]

[27] Increased levels of circulating inflammatory markers in patients with anxiety disorders: a systematic review and meta-analysis. Brain, Behavior, and Immunity | Nielsen, B. M., Werge, T., & Mork, A. (2019)
The relationship between anxiety disorders and inflammation: a systematic review and meta-analysis | Hofmann, S. G., Asmundson, G. J. G., & Smits, J. A. (2018)

lipopolysaccharide (LPS). LPS is an extremely dangerous chemical that has been found to be produced by certain gut bacteria that can enter the bloodstream through a leaky gut. It has been shown through many studies, that the inflammation caused specifically by the immune system's response to LPS can cause both general anxiety and social anxiety[28].

In one such study in rodents, mice that were injected with LPS showed a significant reduction in social behaviour, and mice that already had chronic inflammation (Lurcher mice) showed even greater changes to their social behaviour[29].

Cytokines

Of course, it is not just LPS that can cause anxiety (although it is one of the most serious). Any molecules that break through the barrier of the gut lining into the bloodstream can trigger an immune response.

Once inflammation is activated, the pro-inflammatory cytokines are released. These cytokines usually do a life-saving job of fighting infection in the rest of the body but seem to have a drastically different effect when acting on the brain by altering the way the genes of the brain cells behave. This causes the fear centres of the brain to become overactive and produce anxiety-provoking chemicals like quinolinate, instead of serotonin and melatonin.

---

[28] Lipopolysaccharide-induced cytokine production in obsessive–compulsive disorder and generalized social anxiety disorder | Sjoerd Fluitman et. al., (2010)

Cytokine production capacity in depression and anxiety | N Vogelzangs et.al., (2016)

[29] Hypersensitivity of lurcher mutant mice to the depressing effects of lipopolysaccharide and interleukin-1 on behaviour | Bluthé et. al. [1997]

Cortisol

Another chemical produced, as the pro-inflammatory cytokines interact with the brain, is cortisol. Cortisol, as we saw before, is a chemical that is released from the adrenal glands as part of the fight or flight mechanism. Once cortisol is released, your body becomes primed for action and made ready to fight or run away from danger. This can trigger a severe fear response and possibly even panic attacks when no real danger is present.

In normal fight or flight situations, the cortisol is part of a negative feedback loop, and once the danger is over, the cortisol relays messages to reduce the production of more cortisol. This results in the body "calming down". When a gut microbiota breaks through the intestinal wall and triggers the immune system, however, cortisol is produced through several different mechanisms which can result in the signals to produce more cortisol overpowering the signals to reduce it. This can mean a build-up of cortisol in the body that can create constant feelings of fear or anxiety.

Intolerances

A secondary cause of inflammation from the immune system is when food particles pass through the intestinal wall into the blood stream. This too will trigger an immune response as food particles are also considered "invaders". Bigger problems arise, though, once your immune system becomes trained to recognise a food as a "danger" because it has passed through the gut lining several times. When this happens, the immune system can become hypersensitive to that food and can trigger inflammation every time the food enters the gut and touches the epithelial wall where the immune system is housed. This means that your body will become intolerant to that food and will have an inflammatory reaction every time you eat it. This leads to the situation where certain, normally benign, foods can trigger anxiety without you realising it.

Summary in Plain English

What that all boils down to, then, is that although there are many different and extremely complicated mechanisms of how it happens, the fact is that if you have a leaky gut, bacteria and food particles are going to pass into your blood and trigger anxiety. This anxiety could be constant anxiety, or one-off panic-attacks, and could become triggered by individual foods that you eat and become intolerant to.

What Causes Leaky Gut?

As you can see, Leaky Gut is not a good thing. It has been shown to be the cause of not only anxiety but other mental disorders and autoimmune diseases thanks to the immune response, the inflammation that it triggers, and the previously undiscovered pathways between the brain and the immune system. Although leaky gut is not something that most physicians like to talk about in public, it has been shown to be more common than anyone thought and can be caused by several different things[30]:

Microbiota

If the microbiota in your gut becomes unbalanced (dysbiosis) due to bad diet or antibiotics, and the bad bacteria start to outnumber the good, then caustic materials like bile salts that are usually broken down by these good bacteria can damage the lining of the intestines.

Other bacteria can cause damage to the intestinal wall as well, although it's not entirely understood how. In one study done, it was shown that certain gut bacteria, such as *Escherichia coli*, *Klebsiella pneumoniae*, and *Streptococcus viridans*, increased intestinal permeability[31]. It has also been shown that certain *probiotics decrease* intestinal permeability[32].

This shows that keeping a healthy and diverse microbiota is extremely important, as not only is it possible for pathogenic bacteria to cause anxiety directly through their neurotransmitters, but it is also possible for unhealthy bacteria to cause anxiety indirectly by creating a leaky gut.

---

[30] The prevalence of small intestinal bacterial overgrowth (SIBO) and leaky gut syndrome (LGS) in the general population: a systematic review | Bjorksten, F., Simrén, M., & Monteleone, G. (2017)

[31] Intestinal barrier: An interface between health and disease | Farhadi et. al. [2003]

[32] Probiotics and intestinal barrier function: a systematic review and meta-analysis | Yanfei Zheng et. al.. (2023)

The effect of probiotics on intestinal permeability in patients with irritable bowel syndrome: a systematic review and meta-analysis | Lee, J. W., Park, J. H., Kwon, S. Y., & Lee, J. H. (2015)

Diet

As well as a poor diet negatively affecting your microbiota, which can result in intestinal permeability, there are also certain foods that can directly damage the intestinal wall, such as gluten. This is why celiac disease is so common, and there are probably many more people with slight intolerances to gluten than we realise, because gluten itself can contribute to a leaky gut.

In fact, Dr Kenneth Fine, a pioneer in gluten intolerance research has demonstrated that around 1 in 3 Americans are gluten intolerant to some degree, and 8 out of 10 have genes that could make them prone to gluten intolerance[33].

It should be noted, though, that researchers have also found that a completely gluten free diet can decrease the healthy bacteria in the gut and increase the unhealthy bacteria. This, with most things then, suggests that if you can tolerate it, a small amount of gluten in moderation is the best way to go[34].

I will discuss gluten in more detail later-on when I talk about the good and bad foods in our diets.

Antibiotics

As discussed earlier, antibiotics can lead to dysbiosis, which is the imbalance of the microbiota in the gut. As we have seen this imbalance can lead to leaky gut. This means that antibiotics can indirectly lead to leaky gut.

---

[33] The rising prevalence of gluten intolerance: what's driving it? | Fine, K. D. (2016)

[34] Effects of a gluten-free diet on gut microbiota and immune function in healthy adult humans | Sanz [2010]

NSAIDs

Non-steroidal anti-inflammatory drugs, such as Aspirin, ibuprofen (Advil, Neurofen), and Naproxen (Aleve, Naprosyn), can cause leaky gut as they irritate the stomach and damage the gastroduodenal mucosa. While NSAIDs might sound good as they counteract inflammation, their constant use is counterproductive as they are very likely to cause ulcers and damage the stomach lining leading to a leaky gut. You should steer clear of all NSAIDs unless you really need to use them when prescribed by a doctor.

Stress

Just like with the microbiota, it has been found that chemicals released by stress (such as cortisol) can also damage the intestinal lining and lead to leaky gut, although it may well be indirectly through the microbiota. In other studies, researchers showed that mice that were subjected to stress tests were found to have more permeable intestinal walls than mice that weren't. Again, this gives rise to the possibility of a never-ending cycle—leaky gut causing inflammation that produces cortisol which causes anxiety and which can lead to a more damaged intestinal membrane. It takes a conscious effort to break the cycle and reverse the damage to be completely anxiety free.

Alcohol

Alcohol abuse can damage almost all the organs of the body and the intestinal membrane is no exception. Drinking to excess, which for simplicity's sake could be categorised as drinking over the recommended amount, could lead to a damaged membrane and a leaky gut.

The Wrap-Up

From all the scientific research that I have encountered, it seems undeniable that the gut plays a major role in all kinds of anxiety. It is quite clear that dysbiosis, or an unbalanced microbiota, can cause excessive anxiety, as can leaky gut, and it seems that they can work in tandem or alone to do so.

The good news is that it is also clear that both the microbiota and leaky gut can be repaired and improved by changing the same things. They are both affected by diet, antibiotics, and stress, three things that are within most people's control without having to seek any major help. Before we look at the ways in which we might tackle the repairs, I want to look at how this new-found knowledge of how our gut is causing anxiety issues relates to the questions we addressed at the beginning.

Why is there More Anxiety Now than Ever Before?

With over 40 million people in the US alone suffering from anxiety, it is reasonably safe to presume that there is now a higher percentage of people with anxiety related issues than ever before.

Why would that be?

Well, if an underlying cause for anxiety is the gut microbiota and leaky gut (which I suspect it to be), then the reason for this is simple and is mainly down to the following:

Antibiotics

Antibiotics were only developed at the beginning of the last century, but it is only really over the past few decades that doctors around the world have been handing them out like candy. There is a reason that so many bacteria are now becoming antibiotic resistant, and that is that too many people are being prescribed antibiotics when they don't really need them.

Many doctors are prescribing antibiotics even when patients are suffering from viruses, mainly because it is what patients have come to expect as medicine and feel like they haven't been "treated" if they don't get them.

NSAIDs

These too have become overly popular in the last few decades with very few people realising the damage that they can do to their stomach and intestines.

Some people pop Aspirin every day to lower blood pressure. This is sometimes fine if a doctor recommends it, but all too often people think Aspirin and Ibuprofen are "safe" drugs, while all along they are damaging the stomach lining and causing leaky gut.

Diet

The western diet particularly, with its high gluten, processed foods, junk foods, hidden sugars, and dairy products can cause dysbiosis and leaky gut which, as we have seen, promote anxiety. Although you might argue that the western diet hasn't changed much in a long time, the processing of foods, the addition of preservatives and sweeteners, and the forced growing of seasonal foods all year round have led to a change in what we eat.

It is also only in the past couple of decades that farmers have started to use antibiotics in their animals to "keep them healthy" and make them fatter. This use of antibiotics has, of course, entered the food chain which means that yet again we are all taking in more antibiotics than is needed and playing havoc with the gut microbiota.

Sanitisation

One of the most consequential health trends in western culture over the past few decades has been a preoccupation with cleanliness that borders on the obsessive. What began, understandably, in hospitals has spread throughout the homes and lives of everyone in the western world.

Our paranoia of all things bacterial has seen the rise of antibacterial soaps, wipes, sanitizers, and everything else you can think of. We have made it a mission to make everything around us super clean and bacteria free. This made sense when we thought that most of the bacteria around us were harmful. If we could kill them all then we would surely be much healthier for it. The problem is of course that we now know that not only are many bacteria not harmful to our health, but they are in fact essential to our wellbeing. Our obsession with sanitising the world around us has made it extremely difficult for our microbiota to replenish themselves naturally through the environment. This again has led to a population with unbalanced microbiota, a propensity for leaky gut, and a marked increase in illnesses, such as anxiety and depression.

Anxiety in Other Parts of the World

Similar arguments to those above could be made as to why anxiety is more prevalent in western societies than in eastern societies: The western diet certainly lends itself to dysbiosis and leaky gut more than its eastern equivalent, and antibiotic use in medicine and foods has not been standard practice in the east for as long as it has in the west.

If the diets remain different, we can expect a difference in the number of anxiety cases between east and west to remain, but as the fast-food restaurants pop up in more and more places and the antibiotic use begins to take a measurable toll, we could well see the anxiety gap between the east and the west diminish over time.

Alternative Anxiety Trigger

Although I am primarily looking at Leaky Gut and dysbiosis being the main triggers of anxiety in this book, I feel that I do need to address another major way in which a physical problem with your body could be causing your anxiety—and that way is histamine intolerance.

Histamine Intolerance

You may have heard the term histamine before, especially if you have allergies, but what you may not know is that histamine is a very important neurotransmitter in the body, which, amongst other things, is responsible for stomach acid regulation and brain function. It is also essential in defending the body from invaders, such as bacteria and viruses, as it is one of the first defensive chemicals released from the white blood cells when inflammation is triggered. An important thing to note is that histamine is always present when inflammation occurs in the body.

As already mentioned, you may well know the term histamine in relation to allergies, because when an invading body like pollen enters the body, histamine is the first line of defence to repel the invader and keep the body safe. Unfortunately, for some people the histamine produced during inflammation is more than the body should produce, and it is this excessive histamine production that causes the symptoms of an allergy.

What you may not know, however, is that one of the symptoms of too much histamine is anxiety[35].

So, what can you do?

Luckily for you, this book is about to kill two birds with one stone. If histamine is your problem, then there are two main ways in which you can reduce your histamine levels without resorting to medication:

Reduce the amount of inflammation in your body so the histamine does not need to be produced and eliminate the foods that are triggering your out-of-control histamine production

It just so happens that figuring out what foods are causing the problem, and then reducing unnecessary inflammation through the healing of a leaky gut is what this book is all about. So, if you follow the instructions in this book, you will be automatically tackling a messed-up microbiome, a possible leaky gut, and a potential histamine intolerance all in one go.

Therefore, although the solution in this book is not easy, it is by far the most effective option for tackling your body's physiological anxiety.

---

[35] Histamine and anxiety: a critical review | Hofmann, S. G., Carpenter, L. L., & Smits, J. A. (2016)

Increased serum levels of histamine in patients with anxiety disorders: a pilot study | Bhat, S., Arora, S., Kumar, A., & Singh, R. K. (2019)

The Solution

A Tailored Solution

Hopefully, by now you are convinced that your gut and the billions of bacteria that live in your gut can have a huge impact on your anxiety levels and may well be the actual root cause of your anxiety. At this stage, I should point out that it is unlikely that this is the only cause of anxiety in humans, as the human body is an extremely complex organism, but I do believe it is a major cause of anxiety in many people today and can make beating anxiety through the regular channels extremely difficult for many others. At the very least, I hope I have gone some way to showing you the huge role it plays in anxiety and very probably depression.

The science over the last ten years, since I first wrote this book, has only confirmed my original suspicions and research, and it has proven, at least in my view, the major role that the gut plays in anxiety. I am still of the belief that future studies will cement the idea that the gut plays a major role in many chronic illnesses and will begin to be recognise it as a major way to treat the body for many common maladies and diseases.

For now, while we wait for mainstream medicine to catch up, we need to deal with things ourselves. This means coming up with a solution to treat a leaky gut and balance the microbiota through diet and lifestyle rather than pharmaceuticals, which is a much better solution for the long term anyway.

The problem is, of course, that everybody is different. You have already seen many ways that microbiota and leaky gut could possibly lead to anxiety disorders, and that is just the tip of the iceberg. Each person's microbiome is unique, and their genetic make-up is unique, as is of course their upbringing, environment, and past and present lifestyles. This leads to a completely unique root cause of anxiety. For this reason, it is impossible to just say "Stop drinking sodas and your anxiety will disappear". It may well work for some people but for most people, soda alone will not be the cause of their anxiety.

This may not be what you wanted to hear, and I really do wish that I could give you an easy and clear-cut answer for what you should do to get rid of your anxiety. But I can't, because everybody's answer is slightly different. The good news, though, is that while everybody's details may be different, we have at least distilled the problem down to its fundamental core. We have found the smoking guns, so to speak, and they are the unbalanced microbiota and the leaky gut, and while the specific causes of each might be different for each person, we are at least able to tackle them both based on our knowledge of what affects them.

We know what will keep a microbiome healthy, and we know what will unbalance it and make it unhealthy. We also know what things can cause a leaky gut and what things can help patch it up. With this knowledge, we can tailor a solution that will tackle issues with both the microbiome and leaky gut and get rid of *your* anxiety without ever needing to know the specific details of *your* condition.

This will mean some work on your behalf of course. I am not going to try and tell you that this is going to be some "take 2 pills a day for a week and all your worries will be gone" type of solution. Again, I wish it were, but it's not that simple. The truth of the matter is that tailoring a personalised solution for specific problems means taking a lot of time and a lot of effort. It means being very thorough in keeping track of your progress, and it means being strict and disciplined in following the path to your goal.

If you achieve your goal, though, you will be amazed by the results. Not only could you be anxiety free for the rest of your life, but you could also find you have more energy, better digestion, better skin and hair, and find it easier to lose weight and keep that weight off than you ever have before.

Tailored for You

Identifying the Players

In this game of balancing the microbiota in your gut and trying to repair a leaky gut, there are many players, some good, and some bad. We have already looked at some of the causes of unbalanced gut flora and leaky gut, but now we must look more closely at exactly what foods can help or hinder the quest for an anxiety free lifestyle.

The problem is, of course, that managing the balance of the gut flora is a highly individualised process, as everybody's microbiota is unique, and this makes it very difficult to produce a broad all-encompassing solution to fix it.

This leads us to a more scientific approach where I can guide you in the right direction, but it will ultimately be up to you to define the final solution that will help you cure your anxiety.

I have broken my solution down into 3 phases:

The first phase is the foundation phase and is the simplest route to try and redress the balance of the microbiome. This phase needs to be followed, because it is the basics of a healthy microbiome and gut and is something that everyone should be following all the time to keep the gut and microbiome happy. I believe everybody should follow this phase whether they suffer from anxiety or not. These are the basic things that are needed for a healthy life. You don't need to follow it to the letter, but you should incorporate as much of it in your life as you can. If your problem is just unbalanced microbiota, then phase 1 should be enough to see considerable improvement in your anxiety as you begin to change the balance of power within your gut.

Of course, if you are suffering from a leaky gut then it is unlikely that phase 1 alone will be enough to balance your microbiome and reverse your leaky gut issues. If not, then it is time for you to move on to phase 2 which is much more effective in fixing your leaky gut issues but also much more difficult.

Phase 2 is much more severe than Phase 1 and is basically meant to starve pathogens, yeast, and harmful bacteria in your gut, weed out food intolerances that are triggering inflammation, and rebuild your intestinal wall completely. This is the most effective phase, and the one that will tackle the most cases of anxiety, but it can be extremely difficult to complete for the first few weeks if you are not used to it. It does get easier though, I promise you, and it will not mean you must starve yourself of your favourite foods for the rest of your life. Phase 2 should last 21 days and by the end of this time you should be able to feel the difference in your body and in your anxiety. Hopefully, you should find that your anxiety has completely disappeared. This is where we can start phase 3.

Phase 3 is where things start to get a little easier, albeit very slowly. It is a scientific approach to discovering what foods might be causing any inflammation, and anxiety, by reintroducing them one at a time. By introducing one type of food at a time you can be 100% sure if you have intolerance to that food and that food is an anxiety trigger. If you find you have no problems with that food, then you move onto the next. By the end of phase 3 you will have a list of food types that have an adverse effect on your body and your anxiety, and you can make sure that you never touch those foods again. This way you can stay anxiety free for the rest of your life and enjoy it "like everybody else".

Phase 1 - Redressing the Balance

Phase 1 attempts to redress the balance and increase the diversity of your gut flora without tackling the difficult tasks of repairing the leaky gut membrane or determining a specific allergic response or intolerance. In some people, a simple balancing of the microbiota and an increase in the commensal bacteria will be enough to put a hold on their anxiety without ever needing to take it to a higher level.

Phase 1 involves reducing or eliminating certain foods from your diet to starve the pathogenic bacteria and adding other foods or supplements to help the commensal bacteria thrive. The foods to eliminate in phase 1 are foods that are always bad for the gut and foods that specifically feed the harmful bacteria in everyone and are not dependent on allergies or intolerances.

For the first few months of the process, you should follow phase 1 exactly, as this is the time when your microbiome will be most vulnerable, but this does not mean that you will never be able to have certain foods again. Once you have redressed the balance of your microbiota and rid yourself of your anxiety, then you can be a little more relaxed in your diet control. Of course, you do not want to become so relaxed that you start the problem all over again, but a few indulgences here and there are usually no problem provided there are no intolerances involved (which would be discovered in phase 3).

The Good

Probiotics

We have met probiotics already, as the commensal bacteria that can be purposefully added to the gut to help raise the number of healthy bacteria, and we have seen just how important they are at helping to balance the microbiota and directly reduce anxiety. What we haven't yet looked at is how we can get probiotics and how we can introduce them to our guts. You should try and get as many probiotic sources in your diet as possible.

Fermented Foods

The most natural way to get probiotics into your gut is through non-pasteurised fermented foods. There are fermented vegetables like sauerkraut and kimchi, fermented teas like Kombucha, and of course fermented dairy products like kefir and yoghurt. It is interesting that almost every culture in the world has their own version of a fermented food which shows us the importance of them within our diets. Unfortunately, most fermented foods have been lost in the western diet and the probiotics along with them.

This is another possible reason for the growth of western anxiety over the past few generations, as the art of fermenting foods has been lost. If you can incorporate fermented foods back into your diet, then you will be naturally replenishing your gut with essential and beneficial probiotics.

Although there are hundreds of different fermented foods out there, most are very difficult to obtain in western stores and some rather unpalatable to western tastes. The ones I would suggest seeking out, then, are the ones I mentioned above and are the most readily available in western stores. Make sure when you are looking for fermented foods that they are unpasteurised as pasteurisation will kill the bacteria.

Sauerkraut – I am sure you have heard of this fermented vegetable, as it is the traditional staple German food that you will often find on hot dogs. Sauerkraut literally means "sour cabbage" and is basically finely cut cabbage that has been fermented by various lactic acid bacteria. It is these bacteria that give sauerkraut its probiotic properties.

Fermented Pickles – A simple one to get started on. You can buy many kinds of pickled vegetables these days, or you can make your own. Either way, pickles are a great way to get started with natural fermented foods that contain helpful probiotics. Just make sure they are fermented.

Kimchi – A traditional Korean side dish that is popular around the world and is widely considered to be spicy and sour with a pungent odour. It can be made with many different vegetables and is fermented for extended periods of time. The smell can be quite overwhelming for some people so don't just throw it in the family fridge.

Kombucha – Kombucha is a kind of fizzy fermented tea, originally from China, that is growing in popularity around the world as a health drink. The tea is fermented using a "symbiotic colony of bacteria and yeast", or "SCOBY", and has a huge number of different bacteria in it. You can find Kombucha in many supermarkets these days, but you will also find it in health food shops or online.

Kefir – Kefir is a cultured, enzyme-rich, milk drink that can be made from cow, goat, or sheep milk and is fermented using kefir "grains", which are bacterial fermentation starters. Kefir can usually be consumed by people who are lactose intolerant as the fermentation process consumes most of the lactose rendering it easier to digest.

Yoghurt – As I am sure you are already aware, yoghurt is a food that is also made from fermented milk. In most cases cow's milk will be used. It should go without saying that any yoghurt in your diet should be natural yoghurt and not be mixed with fruit flavourings or sugars. Look for natural yoghurts that say they contain "live cultures" as these are the probiotics you are looking for.

NOTE: Although the fermentation process consumes the lactose that is naturally in milk making it easier to digest, there is another protein in most milk that can cause allergies and help destroy the gut membrane: This protein is called Casein and there are two kinds—A1 and A2. A1 casein is the most common strain found in most cow's milk in the US and Europe, while A2 is found in a small number of cow breeds and most goat and sheep milk.

It has been found that the A1 strain of casein is much more likely to cause allergic reactions, and damage the intestinal lining, than A2 which is why, to begin with at least, I would suggest restricting all milk-based products to sheep or goat milk only or finding a non-animal alternative like coconut milk yoghurt if you can find it.

If you can't find yoghurt alternatives, then stick to a small amount of cow's milk yoghurt. I think the positives of the probiotics will outweigh the negatives of the casein, but it is something to keep in mind if you think you might be sensitive to casein A1.

Supplements

You can also take probiotics as supplements. If you cannot find ways to eat probiotics naturally then supplements might be your best bet. I try to eat probiotics as much as I can through natural means, but I also take a probiotic supplement every day as it is easier, and more consistent, than trying to find fermented foods each day.

Try to find a supplement with as many different strains of probiotic as you can. Most probiotics will contain some form of lactobacillus (usually lactobacillus acidophilus) and a couple of other strains of common probiotic. Getting a supplement with four or five different strains is usually enough, although the more you can get the better.

Another number to look for is the number of cultures in each capsule. A standard amount for regular probiotic products is around 5 billion cultures, which is fine for everyday use without any serious digestive issues. You can always try more cultures if you want but they do get more expensive the more you have. I tend to use supplements with 20-30 billion cultures each, as I have IBS, but these can get quite expensive.

Don't worry too much if you read that most probiotics go straight through your body and into your waste, this is the way it is supposed to be. These are what we call transitive probiotics, and they only need to spend a short time in your gut to make a difference. For one thing, this is why we have so many billion cultures to make sure that some can make a difference, and if you remember that some bacteria only have lifespans of around twenty minutes or so, you can see that the evolutionary time span of the gut is much shorter than we are used to elsewhere.

You should also be aware that many probiotic products need to be kept in the refrigerator or the live cultures inside will be destroyed. Check the label on the supplement before you buy to see if it needs to be refrigerated or not. Not all do, but you might find it easier to get used to doing it anyway just in case.

Prebiotics

We have looked at probiotics and so now it is time to look at prebiotics. Prebiotics are foods that commensal bacteria like to feed on and can help promote the flourishing of these bacteria, which will lead to a strong and healthy gut microbiome. In fact, the original definition of prebiotics was given as *"a non-digestible food ingredient that beneficially affects the host by selectively stimulating the growth and/or activity of one or a limited number of bacteria in the colon, and thus improves host health."*

Prebiotics are just as important as probiotics, because without them the probiotics would not survive, and you need to incorporate them into your diet as much as you can. Many supplements will add some prebiotic in the capsule with the probiotic, which is easy and convenient, but I suggest you try to get as many natural prebiotics in your diet as you can.

The thing that makes prebiotics useful is the fact that 90% of the compounds pass through the stomach and small intestine undigested and end up in the large intestine where they are fermented by the bacteria that reside there. Although this is exactly what we want from prebiotics, as it feeds the commensal bacteria, there is a snag, as it has also been found that the fermentation of these compounds can irritate the bowel in some people and trigger the symptoms of IBS.

This is why, most of the prebiotics I will talk about here are often included in the group of foods called FODMAPs. There are certain schools of thought that believe that FODMAPs are the driving force behind irritable bowel syndrome, and these people have developed diets to help eliminate them completely.

Although I have not experienced much discomfort from eating any of the prebiotics in this list (although I do have problems with broccoli and cauliflower), you should be mindful that there is a small chance that they could trigger a digestive issue which could lead to increased anxiety. I think the chance is very small, and the benefits of eating prebiotics far outweigh this slim possibility, so I would suggest you add these prebiotics to your diet, but keep in mind that, if all else fails, these could be last resort suspects. One way to limit the negative effects that these foods might have, is to make sure you always eat them with other foods and never eat them alone on an empty stomach.

Inulin

Inulin is probably the most common prebiotic compound and is a naturally occurring oligosaccharide, which just means that it is a carbohydrate with 3-10 simple sugars linked together and belongs to a group known as *fructans*. Inulin is found in many commonly occurring foods.

It should be noted that inulin increases the amount of calcium and magnesium that is absorbed by the body, which can be a positive health effect, but means you also need to be careful if you are taking extra calcium or magnesium supplements as too much of them (as with too much of anything) can be damaging.

While inulin has been shown in studies to increase the number of healthy bacteria, like lactobacillus and bifidobacteria, in the human gut, it has also been indicated that too much inulin can also feed the bacterium klebsiella which contributes to leaky gut. This means that inulin is a healthy prebiotic when taken in natural amounts through inulin containing foods but should not be used as an additive to other foods or as a health supplement which many manufacturers are currently doing. You should avoid foods that say they have inulin, or fructans, added as this will not be as healthy as they make out.

It is always better to eat healthy foods than take supplements where possible.

Inulin Containing Foods

- Jerusalem artichoke
- Leeks
- Onions
- Garlic
- Asparagus
- Carrots
- Banana

- Chicory root (high amounts of inulin)
- Dandelion root

Arabinogalactans

Another dietary fibre prebiotic found in food is called arabinogalactans. Like inulin, it is a soluble fibre that reaches the large intestines undigested where it is fermented by bacteria.

Foods that contain arabinogalactans are

- Onions
- Carrots
- Radishes
- Tomatoes
- Turmeric

PHGG

PHGG or *partially hydrolysed guar gum* is probably not something you have heard of before, but it has been undergoing a lot of studies recently in its role as an effective prebiotic for people with digestive issues, such as IBS. Not only has PHGG been found to be a safe and effective prebiotic, but it has also been found to reduce the number of pathogenic *Clostridium* bacteria, which can include such harmful strains as *C. botulinum, C. difficile, and C. perfringes,* and so can help to balance the microbiota[36].

---

[36] Microbiota benefits after inulin and partially hydrolized guar gum supplementation – a randomized clinical trial in constipated women | Waitzberg et al. Nutrición Hospitalaria

PHGG can be found in supplement form in many health stores.

Healthy Fats

Omega-3 and Omega-6 fats are known as "essential fatty acids" because the body needs them for many different functions, but they are not produced by the body. We can only get them from the foods we eat.

Both omega-3 and omega-6 are polyunsaturated fatty acids that differ from each other only in their structure. While they are both essential for different processes in the body, it seems that they are not equally healthy when it comes to inflammation. Omega-3 fats seem to lower inflammation while many (not all) omega-6 fats seem to increase inflammation. This is no problem when the omega-3 and omega-6 fats in our diets are balanced, as inflammation is essential for our survival, but in the modern western diet of processed foods, it seems that the ratio has been skewed towards the omega-6 fats and, in the average American's diet, the ratio of omega-6 to omega-3 fats is over 16:1. This massive increase in omega 6 fats has swung our bodies out of balance and led to a huge increase in inflammation related illnesses, such as anxiety.

Balancing your omega-6 with omega-3 fats to a more natural ratio of about 2:1 to 4:1 would be a huge step in lowering your inflammation and helping reduce your anxiety.

This has been shown in several studies, one of which took 68 medical students and gave them either omega-3 supplements or placebo capsules, that mirrored the proportions of fatty acids in a typical American diet, and then tested their blood on both rest days and exam days. Those students that had received the omega-3 supplements had significantly lower inflammation markers than the control group and marked decrease in anxiety symptoms[37].

These studies are a great demonstration of how a simple change in fatty acid proportions can have a profound effect on inflammation and overall anxiety.

As always, the best way to increase your omega-3 intake is through the foods that you eat rather than supplements.

Foods high in Omega-3

- Fatty fishes e.g., salmon, mackerel, tuna, sardines
- Walnuts
- Almonds
- Flax seeds
- Olive oil
- Rapeseed oil

Foods high in Omega-6

The majority of omega-6 these days is found in processed seed oils and vegetable oils, and they play a large part of the modern western diet.

- Soybean oil
- Sunflower oil
- Corn oil
- Cottonseed oil

---

[37] Omega-3 supplementation lowers inflammation and anxiety in medical students: a randomized controlled trial | Kiecolt-Glaser et al. [2011]

- Peanut oil

Although omega-6 can also be found in high amounts in some whole foods, such as peanuts, these are perfectly fine to eat as they are unlikely to constitute as high a proportion of food intake as processed oils might. For example, it was estimated that soybean oil made up about 7% of the average American's calorie intake in 1999[38] and some people put it as high as 20% today because it is found in so many processed foods.

One thing I would advise is to not obsess over the whole omega-6: omega-3 thing. Both omega-3 and omega-6 acids are essential to a healthy body and so we should be careful not to view one as good and the other bad. If you look online, you will find massive debates on this that go into the finest of details, and many people become obsessed with finding the perfect ratio and amounts to eat. Becoming this obsessed with any part of the food you eat is counterproductive, as we are trying to heal anxiety, not create new ways in which to cause it.

For this reason, then, I would suggest a simple guideline of cutting out as much of the processed seed oils as you can and doing all your cooking with olive oil, or rapeseed (canola) oil, and to eat as much fresh organic fatty fish as you can. Of course, throwing in some almonds or crushed flax seeds now and then, and avoiding processed foods containing soy oil, wouldn't hurt either.

If you make these simple changes to the way you cook and eat food, then your omega-6:omega-3 ratio will start to take on a

---

[38] Changes in consumption of omega-3 and omega-6 fatty acids in the United States during the 20th century | Blasbalg et al. [2011]

healthier balance without you having to stress over everything you eat.

As a last resort, you could always increase your omega-3 intake by taking fish oil supplements, but as always, the real fish is better.

Bone Broth

I am sure you are aware of the almost mythical powers of chicken soup for healing sickness, but what you might not be so clear on is just how much truth is in this "old wives' tale". The secret is in the broth. The bone broth to be exact, and it has been shown to be one of the best foods around for healing leaky gut, improving digestion, and reducing inflammation.

Real homemade bone broth contains a multitude of vitamins and minerals, along with amino acids like proline and glycine, which are not found in significant amounts in the regular meats we eat but are important for a healthy gut and digestion.

The most important parts of a bone broth, though, are the gelatin and collagen that we get from the bones themselves which can help heal a leaky gut while reducing inflammation and promoting a healthy immune system.

Bone broths are ancient foods and are only just coming back into fashion as the superfoods they deserve to be. Although bone broths are good for healing leaky gut, I have added them here in phase 1 because I think bone broths are a food that you should be eating as often as you can for the rest of your life.

To get the full benefits of bone broth, you should not go for the store-bought ones but should make your own, as then you can be sure that there are no additives, and that the broth has been made slowly on a low heat to get all of the goodness from the bones (many store bought ones are created quickly with high heat just to get the flavour). It is quite easy to make, you just need to find somewhere that you can get good quality meat bones. You can use any meat bones that you like—chicken, pork, beef, lamb and fish are all fine—and you can even mix and match if you want, although of course the flavour will change if you do.

There are plenty of bone broth recipes online, but basically you just take a bunch of bones and throw them in a slow cooker with some water and the herbs and spices of your choice (maybe some vegetables) and slow cook them on low for between 12 and 24 hours (closer to 24 if you are using heavy bones like beef). After that you will have a beautiful bone broth that you can drink on its own or use as a stock in other meals. If you want to remove the fat before you eat it then just pop it in the fridge for a few hours, and once the fat has cooled and floated to the top, you can just spoon it off. Just remember that you will be losing some of the nutrients if you remove the fat. Fat Is not always your enemy.

It doesn't get much simpler than that to make your own medicinal food.

Digestive Enzymes

Digestive enzymes (also known as proteolytic enzymes) occur naturally in the body and their job is basically to break down proteins and other food stuffs into more manageable forms for absorption into the blood stream. The two main enzymes created in the body that fulfil this role are trypsin and chymotrypsin, but occasionally deficiencies in proteolytic enzymes do occur and people find themselves with not enough enzymes to digest the food sufficiently. This results in incomplete digestion and solid chunks of food passing all the way through the gut. This can not only result in digestive issues, like IBS, but also malnutrition as much of the food eaten is not properly digested and therefore cannot be absorbed as nutrients.

For people with digestive enzyme deficiencies, adding extra enzymes to their diet can be beneficial in several ways: Firstly, the extra enzymes can ensure that all proteins are properly digested, and ready for absorption into the blood supply, preventing undigested food molecules reaching the intestine and possibly passing through a permeable membrane into the blood and causing inflammation. Secondly, if these digestive enzymes can reach the intestines, then they can also break down some pathogenic bacteria and yeasts that have cell walls made of proteins. If this is combined with probiotics, it can help balance up the microbiota. And thirdly, it has been shown that some enzymes can pass into the blood stream themselves where they can do a great job of "cleaning up" the blood by digesting any rogue proteins that may be floating about trying to cause trouble.

All in all, if you happen to be deficient in proteolytic enzymes, then adding more to your diet might help balance your microbiota and combat inflammation.

Where can you get Digestive Enzymes?

As usual, the best way to add something to your body is naturally, so finding foods with naturally occurring proteolytic enzymes is preferable to taking supplements. Luckily, there are two easy to find foods that are rich in these enzymes:

- Papaya (sometimes called paw paw)
- Pineapple

Papaya contains the enzyme Papain which behaves very similarly to the body's natural digestive enzymes, and pineapple contains the mix of chemicals called Bromelain, which contains, amongst other things, the digestive enzyme cysteine proteinases.

If you can get your hands on an easy supply of papaya, then I would suggest eating a portion before or after every meal to help you with the digestion. If you can't easily get hold of papaya then you could try pineapple, but make sure that it is fresh pineapple and not the canned kind that has been sitting in sugar syrup for a few months.

If getting a regular supply of fruit is not easy for you, then you could always go the supplement route—you can pick up papaya supplements from most health food shops and even on eBay. They even come in chewable form, so you can easily pop one after every meal.

There are people who claim that there is no way that papaya or pineapple can help digestion because they would not survive the surge of stomach acid during digestion. All I know is Papaya has been possibly one of my greatest finds ever for tackling my IBS, as I had great difficulty digesting protein and fat and would feel physically sick after eating red meat or fatty foods, but eating papaya after every meal has made my gut feel almost normal again. I think that eating it shortly after (or even before) the meal means the papaya can help with digestion before the main surge in stomach acid destroys it.

Fibre

Some people advise against eating fibre as it is food for both the good and the bad bacteria in your gut and they see this as an obstacle to redressing the balance. For me though, especially in phase 1, this is fine. In my view, if you are feeding both types of bacteria, then diversity should remain the same, and if eating fibre means that you eat less sugar or processed foods, then it can only be good for you. It also of course "keeps you regular" and keeps the whole digestive process ticking over.

Other Miscellaneous Good Things

Here is a list of other things that you may want to keep an eye on during this phase 1 period, as they have all been linked to anxiety in varying degrees. You probably know that most of these are good for you, but you may not know that they are good for your anxiety.

Magnesium

Most people these days are slightly magnesium deficient, and, if it gets too bad, it has been shown to contribute to anxiety[39]. Adding magnesium through diet is much better than adding through supplements, and it had been shown that it can keep anxiety at bay. Try and add some of the following foods: Dark leafy greens like spinach and chard, almonds, pumpkin seeds, black beans, avocado, figs, and dark chocolate (real dark chocolate i.e. >70% cocoa solids and not the sugar laden pretend dark chocolate).

Calcium

Calcium deficiency is certainly rarer, but it has also been shown to result in anxiety-like symptoms[40]. Magnesium and calcium have a delicately balanced relationship, where too much magnesium can decrease the calcium and vice-versa, so again I would advise making sure that you get calcium from your diet and not supplements. You can also get calcium from dark leafy greens, especially water cress and kale, but you can also get it from cheese, almonds, and broccoli.

---

[39] Magnesium deficiency induces anxiety and HPA axis dysregulation: Modulation by therapeutic drug treatment. Laarakker, M., Singewald, N., de Kloet, E. R., & de Jong, M. (2011)

The Role and the Effect of Magnesium in Mental Disorders: A Systematic Review. Cizza, G., & Fava, M. (2017)

[40] Calcium deficiency and anxiety: A review. Latif, S. A., & Zafar, M. (2020)

The role of calcium in anxiety disorders. Vuong, T. V., & Hieu, T. Q. (2019)

Potassium

Keep your potassium levels high with the following foods: Avocado, spinach, sweet potato, coconut water, banana, white beans, and mushrooms.

Folic Acid

Foods high in Folic acid include leafy greens, asparagus, broccoli, lentils and beans, and avocado.

Zinc

Foods high in zinc include seafood (oysters, crab etc.), beef and lamb, spinach, pumpkin seeds, cashew nuts, dark chocolate, and beans.

Anxiety Super Foods

I hope you noticed that there is some overlap in the foods that are in these lists and some foods contain many of the anti-anxiety minerals. These are what we might call *anxiety super foods*. They include the dark leafy greens like spinach and kale, avocado, nuts and beans. Basically, if you eat as many greens, beans and nuts as you can, you should be fine.

Water

This might seem an obvious one, as anxiety would be the least of our worries if we didn't drink any water, but it is still true that many people today are in a constant state of dehydration, and this has again been shown to lead to anxiety-like symptoms. Basically, if you feel thirsty you are already dehydrated. Drink as much plain water as you can throughout the day.

And no, soda does not make a good substitute.

If you want help keeping track of the foods to eat each day to make sure you get enough of everything you need, then you can download my free anxiety buster checklist at: *http://theanxietyshift.com/bookchecklist*

The Not So Good

Simple Sugars

I am sure you are aware by now that simple sugars are just plain bad for you. You don't need me to tell you that a diet of cakes, candy, and soda is going to leave your body in a less than healthy state, but as well as piling on the pounds, simple sugars are also a veritable gourmet feast for the bad bacteria and yeasts in your gut and are a sure-fire way to wreck the diversity of your microbiome.

As an everyday rule, then, I would suggest steering clear of junk foods like cakes, sweets and sodas as much as you can. Of course, the odd one here and there as a treat won't hurt you, but the fewer the better, and, let's face it, there really is no reason why you need to be drinking soda at all. There is a reason they are well-known as "empty calories". Water is a much more satisfying and healthier alternative to soda.

One thing I want to point out before we move on is that you shouldn't stress out or go all crazy, obsessively checking all your foods to make sure they contain no sugar. This kind of obsession is in no way going to help your anxiety. There will be some things that you eat that contain sugar, and that is probably unavoidable, but if you cut out the obvious culprits like candy and sodas then you will be fine eating foods containing sugar in moderation. Of course, it is not going to help you if you cut out candies, cakes, and sodas only to replace them with high quantities of some other sugary food that perhaps you were unaware had a lot of sugar in it. Here, then, is a brief list of foods that contain high amounts of sugar.

High Fructose Corn Syrup (HFCS)

One thing you should look out for in foods is high fructose corn syrup. Food manufacturers, these days, are using HFCS as the sweetener in their foods because it sounds healthier than sugar or artificial sweeteners. The reality is, though, that HFCS is just another form of simple refined sugar which carries with it the same problems. It is now probably the most common form of sugar used in foods in the US but should be avoided as much as possible. Pathogenic bacteria and yeasts love HFCS just as much as they love regular sugar. Avoid it if you can.

Fruit Juice

This is probably one that you weren't expecting as fruit juice is usually considered very healthy. The problem with fruit juice is that it contains all the sugar of fruit but less of the fibre structure. Eating fruit is healthy because, although the sugar content is high, the fibre of the fruit helps to slow down the absorption of fructose, which is the sugar in fruit. This regulates the blood sugar levels and prevents the spike and crash of blood sugar that can cause anxiety, and that also feeds the bad bacteria.

Commercial fruit juice is usually filtered to remove the fibre, which certainly reduces the health benefits of the fruit. The best way to make fruit juice is to make your own by throwing the whole of the fruit into a blender and blending it. This is still not ideal, though, as blending breaks down the structure of the fibre and reduces its effectiveness. If in doubt, eat the whole fruit and drink water.

Condiments

Although you might not expect it, as they don't always taste sweet, very often condiments and sauces, such as ketchups and salad dressings, contain high levels of sugar. Use sparingly.

Breakfast Cereals

Although often touted as health foods, and honestly, I have no idea how they get away with it, most cereals have huge amounts of sugar in them. Check them out before you buy them.

"Protein Bars"

The shelves are full these days of so called "protein bars" that are marketed as a health food. Unfortunately, they are packed full of sugar and often more than they state on the label. Apparently, only quite recently, a consumer test was done on 103 protein bars, and it found that 60% of the bars tested failed to match their nutrition labels[41]. Many of these bars are no better than your standard candy bar—just packaged differently.

Milk

Milk contains a considerable amount of the simple sugar lactose, with skimmed milk containing more lactose than whole milk. Cream is better, as its lactose content is much lower. Try not to drink glass upon glass of milk, then, although small amounts in moderation are of course fine. If you can use small amounts of

---

[41] "Hidden Sugar in Protein Bars: A Content Analysis of 103 Popular Brands." Katz, D. L., Mellen, A., & Brierley, M. (2019)

cream instead then use it, as is better for you (yes, I know, ironic isn't it)

Trans - Fats

Trans-fats (or Trans fatty acids) are made when manufacturers turn liquid oils, like vegetable oils, into solid fats through the process of hydrogenation, usually to help preserve them and extend their shelf life. Trans-fats can be found in so many foods these days, such as margarine, crackers, candies, cereals, breads, cookies, chips, peanut butters, salad creams and many, many others. You will often see trans-fat on the ingredient label as "hydrogenated vegetable oil" or "partially hydrogenated vegetable oil", as manufacturers know that the word trans-fat is becoming well known for being unhealthy.

As well as clogging up arteries and raising cholesterol with no nutritional value whatsoever, trans-fats are extremely difficult to digest leading to an overworked digestive system and a lack of digestive enzymes. Studies have also found that trans-fats transport lipopolysaccharides to the liver more efficiently than other foods which can alter bile secretion and therefore lead to intestinal membrane damage[42]. Basically, they are bad and should be avoided at all costs; forever.

Thankfully, most companies have stopped using trans-fats because of the health issues, and much of that is due to legislation. However, it is still important to keep your eyes open on the labels.

---

[42] Lipotoxicity: Effects of Dietary Saturated and Transfatty Acids | Estadella et al. [2013]

Gluten

Gluten is a well-known villain in helping to cause leaky gut, as it contains lectins called gliadin which stimulate the production of zonulin in the gut wall cells which creates gaps in the gut epithelial barrier. Zonulin, which was originally discovered by Dr. Alessio Fasano, regulates the "tight junctions" between cells in the gut membrane, and too much zonulin can create a permanently leaky gut[43].

It has also been speculated by some researchers that zonulin can also affect the tight junctions in the cells in the blood-brain barrier, allowing unwanted foreign bodies into the brain.

Gluten is probably a major player in the increase of anxiety in many people today, as it is certainly one of the biggest contributors to leaky gut. For this reason, it should be reduced as much as possible.

Gluten-free alternatives to many foods are popping up these days, as it is becoming trendy to avoid gluten as much as possible. This is a good thing if you carefully check what the substitute is. Many manufacturers do not care about the health of their customers and just want to jump on the gluten free bandwagon. This leads them to add ingredients like soy, or trans-fats, or sugars to the product which makes the food no better (if not worse) than the gluten original.

It should also be noted that gluten has been shown to be an important prebiotic and that completely gluten-free diets can have

---

43 Zonulin and Its Regulation of Intestinal Barrier Function: The Biological Door to Inflammation, Autoimmunity, and Cancer | Fasano [2011]

a negative effect on gut microbiota diversity and can promote harmful bacteria[44].

As we are not looking to repair the "leaky gut" in phase 1, there is no need to illuminate the gluten entirely, but you should certainly try and reduce it if it is a major part of your diet and replace it with other prebiotics instead.

Foods with gluten:

Wheat—bread, pasta, cakes, cookies, wheat-based cereals, brewer's yeast, barley, rye, noodles, crackers, pastries, granola, most sauces (use wheat as thickener).

Processed and Packaged Foods

Unfortunately, the western diet has become synonymous with quick and easy, ready-to-eat, packaged meals; processed meats; instant sides; and fast food. The problems with these packaged and processed foods are too many to mention, as they often contain additives, colourings, preservatives, gluten, soy, hydrogenated fats, trans fats or high fructose corn syrup, and sometimes even all the above. As we have already mentioned, these foods can wreak havoc on the microbiome and gut and should be reduced or eliminated completely, which is difficult to do when they are found in such high quantities in processed foods. Overall, it is much better to stick to natural and homemade foods than relying on the packaged ones.

---

[44] Effects of a gluten-free diet on gut microbiota and immune function in healthy adult humans | Sanz [2010]

Artificial Sweeteners

Yes, I know, I just finished telling you that you shouldn't eat sugar and here I am again telling you that the sugar alternatives are also on the no-no list. And here we thought that they were the healthy alternative. Unfortunately, most new studies show that this is not really the case, and most artificial sweeteners can affect the microbiota just as much, if not more, than regular sugar.

In fact, one of the studies found, that artificial sweeteners (such as saccharine and aspartame) affect the gut bacteria so much that they can cause glucose intolerance leading to high blood sugar, which is, paradoxically, one of the things sweeteners were made to avoid[45]. High blood sugar can then lead to obesity and diabetes. Although high blood sugar is not desirable, it is the drastic effect that sweeteners obviously have on the microbiota that we wish to avoid. It is certainly not clear how the change in microbiota from sweeteners affects anxiety, but it is fair to say that a negative effect of this magnitude is not going to be in our best interests. Therefore, I would suggest steering clear of all artificial sweeteners. If, however, you don't see how you could live without your "sacchaccino", then I would suggest throwing the sweeteners into phase 2 and try reintroducing them one at a time in phase 3 to see how they affect your anxiety. A small amount of natural honey is probably the best bet overall.

If you can live without any of them though, you are better off.

---

[45] Artificial sweeteners induce glucose intolerance by altering the gut microbiota | Suez et al. [2014]

Soy

Soy is possibly the most controversial of foods now, as the old established bandwagon from the 90s that championed the superfood properties of soy has been challenged by the new and increasingly popular bandwagon of painting soy as the evil harbinger of all sickness and death. I would guess that the truth lies somewhere in the middle.

It is true that the push for soy being a health food was done mainly by the huge soybean companies that saw the popularity of vegetarianism and veganism growing and rushed to fill a gap in the market with a protein rich meat substitute. This led to many studies being done, often by the companies themselves, to prove that soy was healthy. What they found proved just that, that soy protein can help lower cholesterol and probably lower the risk of heart disease. This was true and even the FDA put their little rubber stamp to that fact.

The problem was, of course, that most soy products don't just contain soy protein, they contain other things like isoflavones and phytoestrogens, which the soy companies had been quite happy to ignore. It is only now that people are realising that some of these extra chemicals in soy might not have as desirable an effect on the body as people first thought and often are not destroyed through cooking or soaking.

For example, soybeans have been found to contain chemicals like *Trypsin inhibitors,* which interfere with protein digestion and may lead to pancreatic issues. Animal studies have also shown Trypsin inhibitors can stunt the growth of the young[46].

Soy phytoestrogens are another. They negatively affect endocrine function and can cause infertility in women and possibly lead to breast cancer in older women. Not only that, but these soy phytoestrogens can damage the thyroid leading to hypothyroidism and possibly thyroid cancer[47]. Links have also been found between infants on soy formula and the autoimmune thyroid disorder.

That said, after reading a lot of articles on the health benefits and dangers of soy, I am still not convinced either way. There are certainly many sites that breakdown the dangers of eating soy with convincing arguments, and there are also sites that still extoll the virtues of soy as the heart-healthy food it was once considered to be. The problem is, I did not find too many proper scientific research papers with strong experimental data on the dangers of soy. There are studies out there, but they often show weak correlation at best and are inconclusive in my mind.

So why did I put soy in the "not so good" section? Well apart from there certainly being enough evidence overall to warrant a reduction in soy at the very least, there were two studies that caught my attention:

---

[46] Effect of trypsin inhibitor on growth and body composition in children consuming high legume diets. | Chen, J., Wang, Y., Yang, J., & Li, X. (2010)

[47] Soy isoflavone intake and risk of thyroid disease in women: The Nurses' Health Study. | Hankinson, S. E., Willett, W. C., Colditz, G. A., Hunter, D. J., Stampfer, M. J., & Speizer, F. E. (1995)

Soy intake and risk of thyroid disease in men: The Health Professionals Follow-up Study. | Chan, J. M., Stampfer, M. J., Hu, F. B., Rimm, E. B., Willett, W. C., & Giovannucci, E. (2009)

The first was a study done on mice to test the effects of soy isoflavones on anxiety: Obviously, this study was of interest to me, because although there may be other health benefits and dangers from soy, it is only the effects on the gut and ultimately on anxiety that I am concerned about in this book. In this study, researchers fed half of the mice with soy isoflavones and half the mice without. They found that the mice that ate the soy isoflavones exhibited higher anxiety on their tests and showed elevated stress-induced corticosterone (the mouse equivalent of cortisol) concentrations when compared to the mice that did not. The strange thing was, that this only appeared to happen in male mice and not in female[48]. That said, it still demonstrates a significant enough relationship between soy and anxiety (in mice at least) for me to take an interest.

The second study was a human study looking at a whole range of possible effects on the human body of soy and its isoflavones. Most of the tests returned inconclusive results, but when looking at overall adverse effects the report had this to say:

"The most frequently reported adverse events among a total of 3,518 subjects in 49 studies (including 5 non-randomized and 3 pharmacokinetic studies) that reported adverse events were gastrointestinal in nature. These were reported in 33 of 41 comparison studies of soy diets, soy proteins, isoflavones, and phytoestrogen supplements"[49]

The fact that such a large proportion of the studies yielded adverse gastrointestinal (gut) effects was very interesting to me

---

[48] The soya isoflavone content of rat diet can increase anxiety and stress hormone release in the male rat | Hartley et al. [2003].

[49] Effects of Soy on Health Outcomes: Summary | Balk, Chew et al. [2005]

and displays a spotlight of doubt on the health benefits of soy and offers it as a possible gastrointestinal trigger of anxiety.

For this reason, then, I would at the very least cut down on the amount of soy you take in every day. Cutting out the processed foods should help you do this enormously, as a huge number of processed foods these days will contain soy product. Just grab something from the kitchen and look at the label, I bet it has some soy in there somewhere.

Monosodium Glutamate (MSG)

This was a late update to this book, as I have been reading more recently about glutamine, GABA and glutamate. Both GABA and glutamate are essential amino acids for brain metabolism and function, but whereas GABA is an inhibitory neurotransmitter (reduces brain stimulation) and is sometimes known as the brain's "natural Valium-like substance", its partner, glutamate, is an excitatory neurotransmitter (stimulates the brain). This stimulation has been shown to lead to anxiety disorders[50] when the glutamate outweighs the GABA.

Whether glutamate, in foods like MSG, can cross the blood brain barrier and enter the brain is still not clear, but there is certainly a lot of anecdotal evidence of anxiety sufferers who have discovered MSG as a major contributor to their anxiety, and so I would advise cutting out MSG altogether just to be on the safe side. I can certainly attest to this, as I have experienced my own share of

---

[50] The Role of Glutamate in Anxiety and Related Disorders | Cortese, Phan [2005]

MSG "hangovers", and the anxiety it brings is not pleasant. I avoid it as best I can.

Bacterial Die-off

It is important to note, that after about a month of phase 1 you may start to feel a lot worse in your physical health. You may start to feel sick and get stomach cramps. Not everybody does but some do. This is completely natural and is, oddly enough, a good sign, as it shows that the bad bacteria in your gut are starting to die off.

When the bad bacteria die, they often release chemicals that can make you feel bad and might even heighten your anxiety for a time. Don't worry about it, and certainly don't give up, it means that you are winning and are taking back control of your body. It's good to know in advance though, so if you do get it, you will recognise it and not let it derail your progress.

Phase 2 - Elimination

Phase 2 is where the rubber meets the road so to speak. It is the toughest part of the whole process, and one that you may find very difficult to achieve at the beginning. It is also the only way to know for sure what foods are feeding your anxiety. Taking a month to go through phase 1 first will make the transition to phase 2 much easier than jumping straight in, as you will already have made changes to your diet and will have broken slowly from your old routines.

Phase 2, then, is the elimination phase. This basically means that you need to eliminate all foods that you might be intolerant to and therefore could be causing your anxiety. Now to be fair, the list of foods that can cause intolerance is quite large, and this will mean cutting out much of what you would probably consider your usual diet. Just remember that this is not forever, and once you have discovered your triggers, you will be able to eat most of the foods that you used to enjoy with impunity. Would it not be worth a few months of dietary hardship to be free from anxiety forever?

In the full elimination, every food type that has been known to cause intolerance should be cut out of the diet completely for around 21 days. This gives time for the body to adjust to the new diet and the gut membrane to begin to repair itself. You may see your anxiety symptoms get worse for the first couple of days on the diet as your gut reacts to the changes, but after that you should hopefully see your anxiety symptoms subside. Therefore, it is important to be strict with yourself during these three weeks as even the smallest slip-up could jeopardise the entire experiment. If you do see your anxiety symptoms reduce over this time, then it will be a strong indicator that your anxiety is indeed being caused by a leaky gut and food intolerance.

The Challenges

I'm not going to sugar-coat this—the elimination diet is hard. All diets have their own difficulties involved, but the elimination diet can seem particularly challenging, as many of the foods that you can eat may not be foods that you are used to eating. This can mean a complete overhaul of the way you view mealtimes and can mean more time and energy planning and preparing foods in the kitchen.

I would advise you not to eat out too much during the elimination phase, as it is often difficult to know what restaurants are putting in the food you eat, and this could skew your results without your knowing. I would also suggest keeping social dining to a minimum and not travelling during the diet for the same reasons.

It is important that you begin the elimination on a predetermined date and set aside the time to do it with no other engagements that might derail your progress. For this reason, it is also important to discuss the diet with your family and close friends so they understand what you are doing and give you the support that you will need over this time.

What Precautions Should You Take?

If you have a history of anorexia or bulimia, you probably shouldn't follow an elimination diet as the process can trigger the same issues with food that you suffered from before. When eliminating foods, it is easy to become obsessed about the food you eat, so it is important that you view the process as just a means to an end.

If you have a local nutritionist or doctor that you trust, I suggest seeing them before you begin the elimination and discussing with them the diet that you have planned. They will be able to guide you through any possible nutritional issues that might arise and offer any other reasons why you should not follow the diet.

Food Groups to Eliminate

The foods that you must eliminate completely for the first 21 days are those foods that are known to cause digestive distress, leaky gut, or food intolerances. Most of these foods will not be the trigger for you personally, and the majority will have no negative effects for you at all. The problem is that without eliminating these foods, it is virtually impossible to narrow down exactly which foods are causing your anxiety and which aren't.

It should be noted that different specialists recommend different levels of strictness in the elimination of foods. For example, some experts suggest that you cut out almost all the carbohydrates in your diet and eat only fish and certain vegetables. Obviously, this is the most effective method of weeding out the culprits, but it also makes the experience a whole lot more difficult than it should be and is more likely to result in non-completion. Therefore, I would suggest leaving certain carbohydrates in the diet to begin with, specifically those carbohydrates that have an extremely low probability of being the problem food, such as brown/red rice, quinoa, sweet potatoes, and buckwheat. If you come to the end of the 21 days and have not noticed any change in anxiety symptoms, then of course you can begin to eliminate these from your diet and reintroduce other carbohydrates that have already been shown to not be the trigger.

I will put the following foods into a table later so you can see immediately what you can and can't eat.

Gluten

As mentioned in the previous section, gluten is often one of the prime suspects when it comes to food intolerances, and the causes of leaky gut, and so for the elimination diet you will need to cut gluten out completely. This means that you will not be able to eat any wheat products, such as breads, pastas, cereals, and any other manufactured foods that use gluten as an additive (which is many).

Soy

As well as cutting down on soy generally, you should eliminate all soy products during the elimination stage including tofu, miso, tempeh, soy sauce and any foods that use soy as an additive.

Corn

Corn itself is not usually a problem, but with the amounts of genetically modified corn products available today it is often difficult to say if some will be triggers and some not. The chance of someone developing an intolerance to corn is also increased thanks to the amount of corn that is eaten in The States from a very early age, therefore it is better to cut out corn altogether. You should also keep a look out for high fructose corn syrup (HFCS) which is used in an alarming number of products as the sweetening agent. These are purely empty, and anti-nutritional, calories and should be cut out completely as HFCS is the candy that bad bacteria crave.

Meat/fish/poultry

Certain meats can cause intolerances and so should be ruled out during the elimination stage. I found that beef and lamb were both triggers for me so I would include those. Basically, you should rule out any red meats and fatty meats, processed meats (such as baloney, salami etc.) and eggs. You should be safe sticking to chicken, turkey and fish, such as tuna, salmon and mackerel, (just steer clear of any farmed fish that might be high in mercury) but leave out shellfish.

Dairy

Steer clear of cow's milk because of that dreaded casein and stick to products made with rice or nuts or coconuts. This means no milks, yoghurts or cheeses that have been made with cow's milk, unless you really can't find any other yoghurt, then small amounts of cow's milk yoghurt can be eaten for the probiotic value. That is unless it causes you digestive discomfort.

Legumes

Legumes are one of those food types that bring out differing opinions in many experts with some ruling them out completely and some allowing most if not all of them. I have personally found some legumes to be a trigger and so find myself in the eliminating all legumes camp. Legumes are the group of foods that include beans, peas, lentils, and peanuts, that are in fact legumes and not nuts.

Nightshades

You have probably heard of deadly nightshade, but did you know there are many other foods that belong to the same nightshade family? Some of them might even surprise you. Nightshades can be triggers for many people but are often overlooked because they are such common foods.

Nightshades contain *Glycoalkaloids,* which are natural pesticides created by the plant to prevent animals from eating them. These glycoalkaloids bind to the cholesterol in cell membranes and destroy the structure of the membrane resulting in a ruptured cell. In humans, this process can occur in the epithelial cells of the intestines resulting in a leaky gut.

Glycoalkaloids are also similarly structured to cortisol, and so when combined with an excess of cortisol can result in increased levels of anxiety.

So, what are these terrifying nightshade foods? Well, the family consists of potatoes, tomatoes, aubergines (eggplant), goji berries, tobacco, and peppers (bell peppers, chilli peppers, paprika, cayenne etc.) While none of these seem to have anything in common, they all belong to the nightshade family and all produce fruits with a similar little green "hat".

You should cut out all the nightshade foods to start with, although it is much more likely that potato would be an issue over any of the others as the levels of glycoalkaloids reduce drastically in the fruits during ripening and are between five to twenty times less toxic than those found in potatoes. It is important to note, though, that most of the glycoalkaloids in potatoes are found in the skin, so you should remember to peel them when reintroducing them.

Red, green, and yellow bell peppers contain only about 10 mg of glycoalkaloids per kg which is a very small amount and will probably not cause you any difficulty. It should also be noted, that although, for most people, eating any of these members of the nightshade family will pose no problems whatsoever, but as we are eliminating all possible food intolerances, these must be thrown in the hat.

Alcohol

Whether you consider yourself a heavy drinker or not, you should eliminate alcohol from your diet for the duration of your elimination. As discussed before, alcohol can cause and exacerbate leaky gut and so should be avoided until you are sure that your gut membrane has been healed. Alcohol can also affect anxiety directly so going tee-total for a time will ensure that your elimination results are not disrupted. Cutting out alcohol is also a bonus for your microbiota, as the high sugar content in a lot of alcohol is manna to the pathogenic bacteria in your gut.

If you are a very heavy drinker or an alcoholic, then you should discuss with your doctor before you give up alcohol completely for an extended period.

Coffee

Steer clear of coffee. Not only can it irritate the stomach lining and worsen leaky gut, but the caffeine can also affect your anxiety directly and mask the results from the elimination.

Certain Fruits

This is probably one you were not expecting as most people consider fruits to be healthy and full of vitamins. This is partly true, but some fruits also contain other things which can trigger intolerances. One of those things is salicylates, which is a natural defence mechanism of the plant and can be found in particularly high levels in some fruits. Salicylates can irritate the gut membrane and prevent healing of a leaky gut, but there are also many people who have intolerance to salicylates, and one of the major symptoms of salicylate intolerance is anxiety.

Cutting out certain fruits also includes their fruit juices, which can cause more intolerance than the regular fruit as the salicylates are concentrated in the juice along with the sugars, and yet all the healthy fibre from the fruit has been removed.

The fruits with the highest amount of salicylates are as follows:

Apricot, Blackberry, Blackcurrant, Blueberry, Boysenberry, Cherry, Cranberry, Currant (dried), Date, Grape, Guava, Orange, Plum, Prune, Raisin (dried), Raspberry, Strawberry, Sultana (dried), Tangelo, Tangerine.

At a Glance Elimination Food Table

Food Group	Include These Foods	Avoid These Foods
Meat & Poultry	chicken, turkey, all fresh fish (halibut, salmon, cod, sole, trout), wild game, chicken, turkey (free-range, organic) Bone Broth	Beef, pork, cold cuts, sausage, bacon, processed meats, lamb, canned meats/fish, eggs, and shellfish.
Dairy	rice, oat, and nut-milks such as almond milk and coconut milk	milk, cheese, eggs, cottage cheese, cream, yogurt, butter, ice cream, frozen yogurt, non-dairy creamers
Grains and starches	Brown/red rice, oats, millet, quinoa, amaranth, teff, tapioca buckwheat, sweet potatoes	wheat, corn, barley, spelt, couscous, kamut, rye, triticale, pastas,

legumes	None	split peas, lentils, beans, soybean products, peanuts
Nuts and seeds	walnuts, sesame, pumpkin, and sunflower seeds, hazelnuts, pecans, almonds, cashews, nut butters such as almond or tahini	Peanuts and peanut butter, pistachios, macadamia nut
Fruits	Whole fruits	Apricot, Blackberry, Blackcurrant, Blueberry, Boysenberry, Cherry, Cranberry, Currant (dried), Date, Grape, Guava, Orange, Plum, Prune, Raisin (dried), Raspberry, Strawberry, Sultana (dried), Tangelo, Tangerine.
Oils	Olive oil, flax, safflower, sesame,	Butter, margarine, shortening, processed oils, salad

	almond, sunflower, walnut, canola, pumpkin	dressings, mayonnaise, and spreads
Vegetables	Almost all fresh raw, steamed, sautéed, or roasted vegetables	Potatoes (sweet potatoes and yams are fine), tomatoes, broccoli, cauliflower, egg plants, peppers
Condiments	Sea salt, dried pepper, vinegar, Worcesteshire sauce, mustard, most herbs, cumin, turmeric,	Ketchup, relish, chutney, soy sauce, barbecue sauce, salad cream, other condiments, MSG
Beverages	Lots of water, herbal teas, coconut water, kambucha,	Alcohol, caffeine (coffee, black tea, green tea) soda, fruit juice, fruit concentrate, any sugary drink

Anti-Inflammatory Supplements

Healing the leaky gut through a dietary change will put a stop to the systemic inflammation inflaming your brain and causing your anxiety. You can speed this process along by eating foods and taking supplements that combat inflammation and will reduce your anxiety while you are still healing your gut.

Turmeric (Curcumin)

Turmeric is a well-known spice used in Asian cooking for its flavour and vibrant colour. The active ingredient in turmeric—curcumin—has long been known to reduce inflammation and has been used as a health food in The East for centuries. Modern scientific studies also support this ancient practice[51]. If you can find fresh turmeric, then use it in your cooking as much as you can or make fresh turmeric tea. Just bear in mind, that fresh turmeric will stain your hands and clothes worse than any dye you have ever come across.

If you can't find fresh turmeric, or don't see yourself being able to use it that often, then you can get turmeric supplements which you can take two or three times a day to keep your body's inflammation to a minimum.

---

[51] Curcumin Suppresses the Production of Pro-inflammatory Cytokine Interleukin-18 in Lipopolysaccharide Stimulated Murine Macrophage-Like Cells | Renu Yadav et. al. (2015)

Effect of curcumin on proinflammatory cytokines: A meta-analysis of randomized controlled trials | Armita Mahdavi Gorabi et. al (2021)

Turmeric in supplementary dosages can increase irritability in some people, and if you find it affects you in this manner then you can try **grape seed extract** instead.

Taking either of these supplements should decrease your inflammation and your anxiety levels.

Ginger

Ginger, like turmeric, contains very powerful anti-inflammatory compounds called gingerols which have been proven in many studies[52] to reduce inflammation dramatically. Ginger is also good to ease gastrointestinal distress and relax the intestinal tract. Ginger is easy to find and easy to throw in most dishes that you are cooking. You can also drink ginger tea, but make sure it doesn't come with added sugar.

Deglycyrrhizinated Liquorice (DGL)

Otherwise known as liquorice (or licorice) root, this herb has been used for thousands of years for digestive issues, but the modern supplemental form has the glycyrrhizin removed as this can cause high blood pressure.

As well as soothing the stomach[53], DGL can balance cortisol levels, improve acid production and digestion, and help maintain the membrane of the stomach and duodenum.

---

[52] Bioactive Compounds and Bioactivities of Ginger | Qian-Qian Mao et. al. (2019) Effect of Ginger on Inflammatory Diseases | Pura Ballester et. al. (2022)

[53] Gut health benefits of licorice and its flavonoids as dietary supplements | Bharathi Bethapudi et. al. (2022)

Quercetin

Quercetin is a naturally occurring bioflavonoid, found in apples and onions, that acts as a powerful antioxidant and anti-inflammatory. It has been shown to have a positive effect against leaky gut[54]. There is still a lot of research being done on Quercetin, but it is looking good that it will become a major player in the fight against inflammation and leaky gut.

Why Not Eliminate One Food at a Time?

A question I get asked a lot by many people, including my friends, when I talk about this elimination process is "why could you not just eliminate one food at a time from your diet and see if your anxiety goes away? Why must you eliminate all foods at once? Surely this would be much easier."

This is a great question and I completely understand where this idea comes from. It would be much easier to finish the entire process if you only had to stop a single food at a time, and if your anxiety symptoms stopped, then you would have your culprit—simple!

Not so fast. There are several problems with doing it this way, but the most obvious is what will happen if you have more than one trigger? If your anxiety is caused by leaky gut or dysbiosis then the chances are that there is more than one food type that is triggering your anxiety. If this is the case, then let's look at what would

---

Prevention of symptoms of gastric irritation (GERD) using two herbal formulas: An observational study | Russell Setright (2017)

54 Potential Implications of Citrulline and Quercetin on Gut Functioning of Monogastric Animals and Humans: A Comprehensive Review | Victoria Anthony Uyanga (2021)

happen if you had just two trigger foods and tried to eliminate them one at a time.

If you are eliminating just a single food from your diet at a time, then you would eventually come to the time to eliminate trigger food one. The problem is, of course, that eliminating trigger food 1 would not stop your anxiety symptoms, because you would still be eating trigger food two, which would still be causing your anxiety. This would mean that trigger food one would pass as a safe food and be introduced back into your diet. When it came time to eliminate trigger food two, the same thing would happen again— trigger food one would continue to cause the anxiety and so trigger food two would be deemed "safe". This would result in both trigger foods remaining in your diet and you never finding out what is causing your anxiety.

Of course, you could try eliminating one food at a time and leave them out until your anxiety disappears. This could certainly work but would in fact take much longer than a full elimination and is much more likely to fail through error. The problem is that even if you reach a point where you have eliminated all your trigger foods and your anxiety has gone, you then still need to reintroduce each food one at a time to make sure that you catch all your triggers. You cannot just assume that the last food you eliminated was your only trigger.

This means keeping a scientific record of each food you eliminate and then a record of each one you reintroduce. This makes it a much more complicated process and why I haven't recommended it here. Although the full elimination is difficult, it is simple and straightforward and therefore much more effective.

Phase 3 - The Reintroduction

After 21 days, you should be able to see signs that your anxiety has at the very least reduced and hopefully disappeared completely. You will probably still suffer from anxious thoughts and ideas, as these have been hard-wired into your brain over time, but they should feel like they have less weight behind them as they will not have the physically generated fear response giving them more importance than they deserve.

Now it is time to begin reintroducing foods back into your diet one at a time to try and pinpoint which specific foods have been triggering your anxiety. Once you have done this, then you will only have to remove these individual foods from your regular diet to remain anxiety free. It is important when you are reintroducing foods that you do it one at a time and wait a minimum of 3 days after each introduction to allow your body to react.

I would recommend starting with the food that you miss the most, but bear in mind that you should still follow the dietary restrictions in the "Redressing the Balance" section (that means you shouldn't start reintroducing doughnuts). Beginning with the foods you like the most acts as an incentive to get through the painful 3 weeks of the elimination phase and offers a small reward at the end of it. Just remember to reintroduce that food and no other, as you need to make sure you are only testing that individual food.

Once you start reintroducing foods, make sure you keep detailed notes of both the foods you eat and the symptoms you experience. There is a log sheet included with this book to help you keep track of the foods you are eating (see p137) or you can download it from http://theanxietyshift.com/bookworksheets/. If it helps, you could always take photos of the meals you eat and keep a photo log on your phone.

What happens if you get a *Hit*?

What happens if you eat a food, and your anxiety comes back? Well, when you reintroduce a food and see a resurgence of anxiety symptoms you need to stop the introduction of that food, make a note of it in your log sheet and give yourself a break of 3 days where no other foods are introduced. This will give your body time to reset itself before you continue.

The first thing to understand is that you should not discount that food completely just yet. There is a small chance that there could have been other contributing factors to your anxiety symptoms, like an illness, stress, or food contamination. To make sure it is the food that caused the symptoms and not some external factor, you will put that food further back in the list and try reintroducing it again after a few weeks. If you find the same symptoms occur then, it is probably safe to assume that the food itself is triggering the anxiety symptoms, and you would be better off banning it from your diet forever.

If you continue to reintroduce foods over the next couple of months, all the while still following the guidelines of Phase 1 and taking appropriate foods, probiotics, and supplements to help reduce inflammation and heal your leaky gut, then you should find that after about six months you have determined which foods are safe for you to eat and which ones will trigger your anxiety, you have rebalanced your microbiota, and gone a long way to healing your leaky gut.

It may take longer than six months to completely heal your leaky gut, but if you keep to your safe foods and follow the phase 1 regimen, then there should be no reason why your leaky gut won't completely heal over time. It is also about this time that you can possibly be a little more lenient with foods in Phase 1 if you only take them in small doses. For example, if you found that gluten was not a trigger for you, then you will be fine eating gluten in small amounts. You should limit your gluten intake, of course, as it is known to cause or worsen leaky gut, but the odd bowl of pasta here and there, or the odd whole wheat sandwich will probably be fine. Just don't get into the habit of eating bread every day or you could slip back into the same situation you are in right now.

The same goes for the other phase 1 foods like corn and soy and even sugar. In moderation, they will be fine and if they are outnumbered by healthier foods in your diet, then you should be golden.

Getting to this stage is a bit of an ordeal, I know, but I promise you it is worth it, and you will feel better in so many ways. Just try and keep the end goal in mind and remember that it is only a very small amount of time compared to the rest of your life and surely worth a bit of discomfort if it means you live the rest of that life anxiety free.

You may even find new foods that you like and new dishes that you have never tried before. You might even enjoy the ride. Best of luck.

Exercise

As well as maintaining a healthy and fit body, exercise can also help build mental fitness, and it has been shown in many studies that exercise can reduce stress and anxiety.

There are both short and long-term benefits to the brain to be had with regular exercise. The short-term benefits can be felt immediately and are through the release of chemicals like endorphins. Endorphins are natural painkillers and are what allow long distance runners to break through the "pain barrier". These, and other short-term chemicals released in the brain during exercise, can give a positive feeling, and reduce stress and anxiety, hours after exercising.

The long-term benefits include the actual growing of new blood vessels in the brain and increased levels of brain derived neurotrophic factor (BDNF), which has been found to be reduced in anxiety sufferers in some studies.

Another long-term effect of exercise is the formation of neurons in the brain that are specifically designed to release the neurotransmitter GABA that basically inhibits brain activity making sure that neurons don't fire when they shouldn't be firing, and effectively reducing anxiety.

In one study, researchers found that those who got regular vigorous exercise were 25 percent less likely to develop depression or an anxiety disorder over the next five years[55].

---

[55] Exercise for Mood and Anxiety: Proven Strategies for Overcoming Depression and Enhancing Well-Being 1st Edition | Otto, Smits

In another study[56], researchers took some mice and put half of them to work on the treadmill, and the other half were allowed to lounge around with no exercise at all. They found that the half that had done the exercise had notably more newly formed neurons in the brain and specifically the neurons that released GABA. They then wanted to see how the GABA would affect the anxiety of the mice directly, so they immersed all the mice in cold water, something that mice find particularly distressing (not only mice I would imagine). What they found was that the mice that had exercised experienced much shorter periods of anxiety when compared to their more sedentary counterparts, as the GABA moved quickly to dampen the firing of the specific neurons for too long.

It is evident, then, that exercise is good for combatting anxiety and should go hand-in-hand with any anxiety regime that you try, including this one. Remember, the aim here is not to develop a short-term process to temporarily quiet your anxiety, but to create a whole new lifestyle, and set of habits, that will keep you anxiety free for the rest of your life. Exercise is an important part of that lifestyle.

Now before you start panicking and the thought of spending hundreds of dollars on gym memberships and hours a day on the treadmill make you jack the whole thing in, please remember that exercise does not have to be a scheduled and structured activity. Exercise can be as simple as going for a walk instead of driving or taking the stairs instead of the elevator. If you can muster around

---

[56] Physical exercise prevents stress-induced activation of granule neurons and enhances local inhibitory mechanisms in the dentate gyrus | Schoenfeld et al. [2013]

150 minutes of exercise a week, then you are on the right road for a healthier body and brain. That's about 20 minutes per day, and if you can break that into two 10-minute walks, you will barely notice it. But your brain will.

Meditation and Mindfulness

In previous chapters, we have looked at how stress can cause anxiety through the release of cortisol and other chemicals. Keeping stress levels to a minimum is an essential part of maintaining an anxiety-free lifestyle.

One way to reduce stress naturally is to practice meditation of some kind. There are many types of meditation and each of them can be useful in a fight against anxiety. The easiest form of meditation for anxiety, which could be argued is not really a form of meditation at all, is mindfulness.

Mindfulness is simple because it can be done anywhere and at any time and does not need any special equipment to do it. It is simply concentrating the attention and awareness on the present moment—the here and now—instead of worrying about what happened yesterday or what will happen tomorrow. Practicing mindfulness helps to keep your mind on what is happening right now and there is very little to worry about in the right here and the right now.

The ins and outs of mindfulness and meditation are way beyond the scope of this book, but I would encourage you to look for information elsewhere and try it for yourself.

In Closing

I truly believe that if you follow this process and balance your bacteria and heal any issues with your gut, then you will be on the fast-track to being able to beat your anxiety for good, and, at the very least, you should find that the overall levels of your anxiety will be noticeably reduced.

It certainly did wonders for me, so I know it works.

Sure, I still have thoughts and anxious fears that crop up every now and then, and you will too, because these are locked away in the long-term memory and will pop up whenever their trigger appears, but once you have healed your body you will find it so much easier to tackle these rogue thoughts without the backdrop of inflammation cranking your fear response to 10.

If you find you need a bit of help in overcoming these thoughts, then I would suggest a bit of Cognitive Behavioural Therapy (CBT) as it is great at combatting those errant thoughts that pop into your head uninvited and stir the fear response up again.

Therefore, as I mentioned at the beginning, I advise a two-step system of healing the body and then the mind. Once you have completed a gut rehab, you will have healed your body and will find it much easier to heal your mind. If you can do the two at the same time, then even better.

If you don't fancy heading to a therapist for an official dose of CBT then look out for my second book in The Anxiety Shift series which will give you some simple, straightforward, and actionable CBT techniques to help you rid yourself of those unwanted thoughts and reset your brain to the way you want it.

It's also important to remember, of course, that some anxiety is healthy and completely normal, and you will never get rid of anxiety from your life completely.

If you can get it down to "normal" levels, so it has very little impact on your day-to-day life, then you will have been successful.

Beating out of control anxiety is a realistic target, and it certainly does take a combination of lifestyle changes, but if you start by tackling your gut first it will put you in a great position for building other positive habits that will keep you anxiety-free for the rest of your life.

Good Luck.

Worksheets

To download the free worksheets that accompany *The Anxiety Shift* book series, please head to:

https://theanxietyshift.com/bookworksheets/

Please also come along and join my Facebook group at https://www.facebook.com/anxietypanicdisorders/

If you are now ready to tackle your anxious thoughts, then you can check out the second book in The Anxiety Shift series specifically aimed at tackling the anxiety in your mind: The Anxiety Shift – Mind Reset. Find it on Amazon now, or get the link at https://theanxietyshift.com

My new book is also available now called: The Anxiety Gap - Between Hope and Fear. It offers a visual representation of anxiety to help you understand your anxiety more easily and therefore help you beat it using a more thorough approach. Find it on Amazon.

7 Day Meal Log and Symptom Sheet

	Morning Foods	Symptoms	Afternoon Foods	Symptoms	Evening Foods	Symptoms
Day 1						
Day 2						
Day 3						
Day 4						
Day 5						
Day 6						
Day 7						

Introduced Food Symptom Log Sheet

	Food Introduced	Day 1 Anxiety	Day 2 Anxiety	Day 3 Anxiety
1				
2				
3				
4				
5				

Other Sources

Non-notated Sources

- http://articles.mercola.com/sites/articles/archive/2012/03/18/mcbride-and-barringer-interview.aspx
- http://perfecthealthdiet.com/2010/07/bowel-disease-part-ii-healing-the-gut-by-eliminating-food-toxins/
- http://www.ncbi.nlm.nih.gov/pmc/articles/PMC3179073/
- http://www.lef.org/protocols/health-concerns/chronic-inflammation/Page-01
- http://japr.oxfordjournals.org/content/18/2/367.full
- http://www.scielo.br/pdf/pn/v3n1/v3n1a02
- http://www.drkaslow.com/html/leaky_gut.html
- http://syontix.com/the-gut-brain-axis-how-endotoxemia-and-leaky-gut-impact-the-hypothalamic-pituitary-adrenal-axis/
- http://www.flyfishingdevon.co.uk/salmon/year2/psy221anxiety/psy221anxiety.htm
- http://www.ncbi.nlm.nih.gov/pmc/articles/PMC3023594/
- http://articles.mercola.com/sites/articles/archive/2013/06/20/gut-brain-connection.aspx
- http://www.apa.org/monitor/2012/09/gut-feeling.aspx
- Microbial Endocrinology: The Microbiota-Gut-Brain Axis in Health and Disease – Lyte & Cryan

- http://www.cag-acg.org/uploads/cddw2013/2013_2presentations/gut_brain_ibs_axis_verdu.pdf
- http://www.functionalmedicineuniversity.com/public/Leaky-Gut.cfm
- http://articles.mercola.com/sites/articles/archive/2009/11/10/Dietitian-Says-Eating-Right-Is-Best-Way-to-Optimize-Good-Gut-Bacteria.aspx
- https://www.psychologytoday.com/blog/evolutionary-psychiatry/201404/the-gut-brain-connection-mental-illness-and-disease
- http://www.healthline.com/health-news/mental-immune-system-cells-trigger-anxiety-in-the-brain-091713
- http://onlinelibrary.wiley.com/doi/10.1046/j.1440-1746.2003.03032.x/full
- https://login.medscape.com/login/sso/getlogin?urlCache=aHR0cDovL3d3dy5tZWRzY2FwZS5jb20vdmlld2FydGljbGUvNzExODY3&ac=401
- http://www.therootofhealth.com/healing/
- http://chriskresser.com/9-steps-to-perfect-health-1-dont-eat-toxins/
- http://psychcentral.com/news/2008/10/28/anxiety-may-be-linked-to-immune-system/3212.html
- http://onlinelibrary.wiley.com/doi/10.1046/j.1440-1746.2003.03032.x/full
  - http://www.nytimes.com/health/guides/symptoms/stress-and-anxiety/the-body's-response.html